Downtown Chicago's Historic Movie Theatres

ALSO BY KONRAD SCHIECKE

Historic Movie Theatres of Wisconsin: Nineteenth Century
Opera Houses through 1950s Playhouses, Town by Town
(McFarland, 2009)

Historic Movie Theatres in Illinois, 1883–1960
(McFarland, 2006)

Downtown Chicago's
Historic
Movie Theatres

KONRAD SCHIECKE

McFarland & Company, Inc., Publishers

Jefferson, North Carolina, and London

All photographs are courtesy of the Theatre Historical Society of America unless otherwise noted.

LIBRARY OF CONGRESS CATALOGUING-IN-PUBLICATION DATA

Schiecke, Konrad, 1938–
Downtown Chicago's historic movie theatres / Konrad Schiecke.

p.   cm.
Includes bibliographical references and index.

ISBN 978-0-7864-6590-3
softcover : 50# alkaline paper ∞

1. Theaters — Illinois — Chicago — History.
2. Motion picture theaters — Illinois — Chicago — History.
I. Title.

PN2277.C4S35 2012   384'.850977311—dc23   2011034479

BRITISH LIBRARY CATALOGUING DATA ARE AVAILABLE

Front cover image: Postcard of Chicago Theatre,
Chicago, Illinois, Max Rigot Selling Co. (n.d.)

Manufactured in the United States of America

*McFarland & Company, Inc., Publishers
Box 611, Jefferson, North Carolina 28640
www.mcfarlandpub.com*

Table of Contents

Acknowledgments

The impetus for this book began with the permission from the Theatre Historical Society of America to use some photographs from their archives to enhance the story of Chicago's downtown movie theatres. I am exceedingly grateful to Karen Colizzi Noonan, president, and Richard J. Sklenar, executive director, for their support.

The Theatre Historical Society of America (THS) is the only organization in the United States that records and preserves the rich architectural, cultural and social history of America's theatres.

Located in Elmhurst, Illinois, west of Chicago's Loop, above the historic York Theatre, THS makes available information on more than 15,000 theatres, primarily in the United States, through its collections and publications. Also housed there are the American Theatre Architecture Archive and the American Movie Palace Museum.

Photographs of the movie projectors, including the Mutoscope, and the photograph of the facade of the Central Music Hall are from the Tom Watson Collection, with the kind permission of his son, John.

A unique website (www.chicagopc.info) has permitted the use of the Strand Theatre photographs. Primarily in postcard views, the website provides an archive of images of historic Chicago buildings.

Author Eric Bronsky has graciously permitted the use of the photograph of the Gem Theatre on South State Street in 1941.

Current photographs of theatres open in Chicago's revitalized downtown, including the Randolph Street playhouses, are from the author's collection.

Introduction

The story of Chicago's downtown, from its early development through its struggles and restoration, is mirrored in the history of the movie theatres that occupied its streets. Chicago's downtown theatres have reflected a growing city, pictures from the past filled with promise and reinvention.

Downtown, the central business district, includes the area bounded on the west and north by the Chicago River, on the east by Lake Michigan, and on the south by Roosevelt Road (1200S). In 1897, an elevated rail loop was completed in downtown Chicago; this is the reason the center of the city is commonly referred to as "the Loop." The term refers to an area bounded by a public transit circuit along Lake Street (200N) on the north, Wabash Avenue (44E) on the east, Van Buren Street (400S) on the south, and Wells Street (200W) on the west.

This book presents the chronological tale of Chicago's theatres as they opened after the Great Fire of 1871. This is the best way to present the theatres, especially as a way to understand how they evolved. An alphabetical listing of the theatres can be found in Appendix B.

Chicago was a bustling town in the mid–1800s, particularly its downtown. State Street, its main street, was lined with a hotel and numerous retail establishments. Early downtown theatres featured a variety of entertainments: vaudeville, minstrel shows, and legitimate theatres offering the latest theatrical stage productions. The Great Chicago Fire of 1871 consumed the central business district leveling hotels, department stores, Chicago's city hall, the opera house, theatres, and churches.

New plans for the future were formed quickly; Chicago had lost none of her old spirit. The city fathers knew places of amusements would be last on the list to be rebuilt so James H. McVicker, a popular Chicago actor, took it upon himself to rebuild his theatre. It would be the first theatre to open within a year after the fire. The McVicker's became early Chicago's most popular theatre. During the following two decades Chicagoans were treated to dramas, musical comedies, vaudeville, opera, and concerts at newly built theatres and music halls. Dime museums and penny arcades became popular as well.

Hotels, department stores, office buildings, and restaurants sprouted up along State Street. With the rebuilding of downtown Chicago came a new kind of architecture from which the skyscraper would evolve. Two of the architects of the First Chicago School included Dankmar Adler and Louis Sullivan who not only had significant influence upon architecture, but transformed the future of the theatre; theatre historian David Naylor calls their Auditorium "the most pertinent nineteenth-century building to the development of movie palaces" (Naylor, *American Picture Palaces*).

During the first decade of the twentieth century, the first nickel theatre to feature the new technology of "moving pictures" opened in the Palmer House block on State Street. Moving pictures had appeared in the 1890s at the end of a vaudeville program. The penny arcades featured moving images on early, individually viewed machines like the Kinetoscope. Downtown's popular playhouses presented programs showing the new pictures.

Soon the early silent movie theatres replaced the dime museums and penny arcades, attracting people to Chicago's center. As the picture craze began to catch on, theatres began to multiply, with the number of movie theatres doubling by the beginning of the next decade.

Chicagoans saw the most wondrous movie palace in the world, the Chicago Theatre, open in 1921. The theatre's large vertical sign was to become the symbol for the city itself. Throughout the 1920s grand movie palaces were built in downtown Chicago, and by the 1930s, there were more movie theatres downtown than in any other part of Chicago.

The perfection of sound synchronized to film movement brought an end to the silent movie era in the late twenties. Theatre owners soon realized that people wanted to see the "new films that talked" and converted their projection equipment to sound capabilities. Those owners that could not afford the high costs of such an undertaking soon closed their doors.

The Great Depression put a halt to the building of enormous theatres. Only one new theatre opened downtown in the 1930s, a theatre devoted entirely to newsreels. When America sent soldiers into combat during World War II, people attended the movies for reports on the war.

In addition, as television became popular, attendance at the movies dropped. People moved to the suburbs. Downtown Chicago began to lose large numbers of retail customers to the newly built suburban shopping malls, resulting in the birth of the suburban multiplex. Shoppers could now see a movie in one of the many small, narrow theatres, usually part of the shopping mall. State Street had lost its preeminence to both the suburbs and North Michigan Avenue.

Part of post-war improvement programs such as building a subway under downtown with separate entries into ten large retail stores were intended to make State Street shopping more enjoyable. Downtown movie palaces introduced bigger screens and color with new technical processes called 3-D, Cinerama, CinemaScope, Todd-AO, and VistaVision, to name a few. Hollywood was reacting to black-and-white television. Efforts to entice people back downtown eventually failed.

Some upscale merchants moved to Michigan Avenue with film exhibitors following along. Those movie theatres that remained open often featured films with adult themes of sex and violence. Instead of staying downtown after work to have dinner and go to a show, people left for the suburbs. Downtown Chicago had become a dismal place.

In 1989, the remainder of the block bounded by State, Dearborn, Washington, and Randolph Streets was razed as a result of urban renewal plans. It came to be called Block 37. The Roosevelt Theatre was the first to be demolished, the United Artists when the entire block was leveled. The Woods Theatre closed that year; Chicago's Loop was without a movie theatre for the first time since the beginning of the century.

At the start of the twenty-first century, Block 37 still stood empty. Some saw this space as a mirror to the past, the potential for Chicago's downtown to rebuild and rise again. In 2008, some plans became a reality. An office tower opened along with the new WBBM-TV street-front studio and offices. A five-story, glass-enclosed mall opened in late 2009.

The Gene Siskel Film Center moved to a new theatre on State Street in 2001. "*State Street, that great street*" began to blossom again, this time by bringing back to life its historic movie palaces — the Chicago, Oriental, and Palace — restoring them to complement the other live entertainment venues open downtown to provide theatregoers with new and exciting stage productions, operas from Chicago's Lyric Opera, and concerts by Chicago's renowned symphony orchestra.

So it might be said that Chicago has come full circle. The city has saved some of its most luxurious movie palaces not by showing films but by presenting stage productions. And the story of these theatres remains alive, while downtown Chicago once again reinvents itself.

Part I

HISTORICAL OVERVIEW

1. Early Amusements

In the mid-nineteenth century, Chicagoans could find a variety of entertainments downtown: minstrel shows, dramas, musical comedy, vaudeville, penny arcades, and burlesque. The opening of the Rice Theatre on the south side of Randolph Street between Dearborn and State Streets on June 28, 1847, marked the beginning of drama in Chicago. The frame building was constructed for theatrical productions. It burned down in 1850 and was rebuilt of brick, reopening in 1851. Larger and more elegant was the McVicker's Theatre, which opened on Madison Street between State and Dearborn streets. The McVicker's was built by Mr. James H. McVicker, a popular actor, and opened on November 5, 1857, on the thirtieth anniversary of the city of Chicago. People preferred the newer theatre, and business fell off at the Rice Theatre causing the owner to have it demolished in 1861. Chicagoans in 1866 could choose from three places of amusement: the McVicker's Theatre, Col. Wood's Museum on the north side of Randolph between Clark and Dearborn streets, and Emerson and Manning's Minstrels on the east side of Dearborn Street near Randolph Street (*Chicago Daily Tribune*, 21 October 1935).

The Chicago Fire of October 1871 swept away the central business district, leveling hotels (the new Palmer House Hotel had been open for only two weeks), department stores, Chicago's city hall, offices, banks, opera houses, theatres, churches, and public works. However, the city started to rebuild almost immediately, "just as soon as bricks were cold after the fire." Six months after the fire, the *Chicago Daily Tribune*, in its progress reports of the rebuilding efforts, wrote "New plans for the future are continually formed that show Chicago has lost none of her old spirit" ("New Chicago," *Chicago Daily Tribune*, 14 April 1872). The city fathers knew that places of amusements would be last on the list to be rebuilt, but two actors, James McVicker and Frank Aiken, took it upon themselves to start rebuilding the theatres. Richard Hooley and Sam Myer followed, also establishing new theatres.

The McVicker's Theatre was rebuilt on the same site within one year after the fire, opening on August 20, 1872. By the end of 1872 in downtown Chicago, audiences were tempted with drama and comic opera at Hooley's Opera House, "Laughable Burlesque" at Myer's Opera House, and variety shows at Aiken's Theatre.

After the first theatres reopened, Chicago's leading businessmen met in September of 1872 to discuss the building of a Grand Opera House. Mr. James McVicker felt "it would have a positive benefit in awakening a general appetite for amusements. An unusual attraction at one has the effect of stirring up business for all." The businessmen felt that it also would have a positive effect on the city's commercial prosperity. That same month the Chicago Musical College opened at 493 Wabash Avenue, the enlarged continuation of the Chicago Academy of Music.

By the next year the *Chicago Daily Tribune* called Chicago the best "show town" in America. "People visited one or more of the theatres each week." In reviewing the "amusements" to the end of the 1870s, the McVicker's and Hooley's remained among the leading playhouses. (Myer's and Aiken's had closed their doors.) Hooley's at one point was called "the Parlor Home of Comedy" presenting the comic operas of the English Opera Company. The McVicker's offered the light comedy *Saratoga* and plays by Shakespeare. Also popular were Hamlin's and Haverly's theatres, each known for their presentations of "minstrelsy." And during this time, the New Chicago Theatre (formerly Kingsbury Hall) featured dramas and operettas.

During the 1880s and 1890s, the *Chicago Daily Tribune* showcased some of the newly built playhouses. The "Gay Nineties" in Chicago were considered the golden age of the stage. Romantic dramas, musical comedies, and melodramas remained the highlight of the two decades at the McVicker's, Schiller, Grand Opera House, Dearborn, Clifford's Gaiety, Hopkins, and Studebaker theatres. The Chicago Opera House, Olympic, and Columbia presented vaudeville, comic opera, and "artistic burlesque." The Olympic Theatre was one of the most popular variety theatres, advertised as "Chicago's model variety theater" offering "continuous vaudeville" along with the Chicago Opera House. Hooley's presented Humperdink's fairy opera *Hansel and Gretel*. In October 1898, the Four Cohans headed the bill at the Olympic. (They would later own the Grand Opera House.) Operas were performed on stage at the Auditorium, with the Central Music Hall and Steinway Hall offering concerts, recitals, and lectures. One could view the National Panorama Company's *Battle of Gettysburg* at Wabash and Hubbard Court in the circular building that would become Cleveland's Theatre and then the Strand Theatre.

Mr. McVicker maintained his opinion

that "the more first-class theatres there were in a metropolitan city, the better for its general prosperity" ("Amusements," *Chicago Daily Tribune*, 9 October 1872).

Chicago School of Architecture

After the Great Chicago Fire of 1871, the city's recovery began the day the final flame was extinguished. Potter Palmer secured a loan and rebuilt his hotel in a lot across the street from the original, proclaiming it to be "the World's First Fireproof Building." Just a decade after the fire, Chicago became the second-largest city in the country, and a new kind of architecture emerged that is often called the Chicago school of architecture. This was the golden age of building in Chicago (Condit, *The Chicago School of Architecture*).

Architects Daniel H. Burnham and John W. Root built upon architect Frederick Baumann's ideas that called for each vertical element of a building to have a separate foundation that ended in a broad pad, thereby distributing the weight over the marshy land on which Chicago was built. This type of foundation was used in their ten-story Montauk block (1882) on West Monroe Street, often considered the first skyscraper.

For their Auditorium building in 1889, Dankmar Adler and Louis Sullivan took these ideas further. Adler had experience as an engineer with the Union army during the Civil War and devised a "raft" of timbers, with steel and iron I beams, to "float" the Auditorium. For historian David Naylor, the Auditorium is the "most pertinent 19th-century building to the development of movie palaces in its double-shell construction." The forerunner to the Auditorium was Adler's Central Music Hall at State and Randolph streets completed in 1879. It was a combination of traditional masonry-bearing walls and internal iron members.

The architecture of Henry Hobson Richardson was a source of inspiration to

Chicago architects. His Marshall Field Wholesale Store that filled the block bounded by Adams, Quincy, Wells, and Franklin streets influenced the design of Adler and Sullivan's "Richardsonian-Romanesque" inspired Auditorium. Also influenced by these designs was Solon S. Beman for his brick and granite Studebaker Building (Fine Arts Building) on Michigan Avenue to house both the Studebaker Theatre and the World Playhouse (placed on the National Register of Historic Places in 1975).

The nature of steel provided another source of inspiration. Completed in 1892, Burnham and Root's Ashland block on the northeast corner of Clark and Randolph was a mixture of Romanesque features (the large rounded archway of the Clark Street entrance) and the simplicity of the Chicago school (rounded corners and curved bays from floors four to fifteen). The Olympic Theatre, later called the Apollo, occupied this site from 1895 to 1949 when it was demolished for a bus station.

These first architects would have a profound influence upon architecture. Beginning in the early 1880s, they pioneered steel-frame buildings with masonry cladding (usually terra cotta), allowing large plate-glass window areas. These early buildings were the first modern skyscrapers.

Vaudeville

Before the turn of the century, vaudeville was one of the most popular forms of entertainment. Vaudeville programs presented interchangeable acts without a connective story tying them together: dancers, singers, acrobats, jugglers, magicians, comedians, and even animal acts appeared on the vaudeville stage. Vaudeville in part developed from other popular amusements of the mid-nineteenth century known as dime museums, concert saloons, minstrel shows, and variety theatres. The dime museums combined "un-

usual" exhibits with variety shows featuring specialty acts common to minstrel shows.

Messrs. Charles E. Kohl and George Middleton opened the first vaudeville entertainment in 1882, and in the following year they opened the Globe Dime Museum downtown. These two circus men would become the early leading vaudeville theatre chain in Chicago. Vaudeville increased in popularity, and Kohl and Middleton's success allowed them to lease the Olympic Theatre with George Castle as manager. They then leased the Chicago Opera House in 1895, presenting continuous vaudeville in both theatres (Gomery, *Shared Pleasures*).

Kohl and Middleton dissolved their old dime museum and theatrical firm on September 29, 1897. In 1900, Kohl bought out Middleton's leases to partner with George Castle to build the Majestic Theatre. Kohl and Castle never went national and sold out to the Orpheum Circuit.

The Orpheum and Keith-Albee circuits were national vaudeville chains and dominated big-time vaudeville. Edward F. Albee and Benjamin F. Keith introduced the continuous show format where performers continued in a cycle without emptying the theatre after every show. Their motto was "Come when you please; stay as long as you like." When legitimate theatres in the last decades of the nineteenth century were charging $1.00 to $1.50, vaudeville entrepreneurs opened new low-priced playhouses known as "10–20–30" theatres, where ticket prices ranged from ten cents to thirty cents (Gilbert, *American Vaudeville*).

Vaudeville would be transformed when the Orpheum Theatre was built in 1907 by Jones, Linick and Schaefer. Said to have one of the most beautiful facades in Chicago, the Orpheum offered "continuous vaudeville" from morning to night. At the same time, these men began opening smaller photoplay houses in the Loop, where the "old kind" of vaudeville could be presented along with the moving pictures. By the end of the nineteenth century, movie presentations as single acts in vaudeville theatres had become an established pattern. Vaudeville managers often placed these moving pictures as the last act. Vaudeville spread the appeal of the new moving pictures, but in doing so foretold its end. The "talkies" and the Great Depression proved to be the end of vaudeville.

In addition, there were small-time vaudeville houses and, usually for a lower admission, burlesque houses. In the early days, burlesque was distinguished from vaudeville acts by skits that usually mocked the social attitudes of the upper, wealthier classes. Parodies of popular theatre plays were referred to as burlesques as well. Early burlesque houses were thought of as stepping stones for comics such as Jack Benny, Milton Berle, and Red Skelton. These comedians were often the first act of the program. Eventually, burlesque became a genre of adult entertainment and bore little resemblance to the famous early days of vaudeville.

At the turn of the century, State Street south of Van Buren Street was often referred to as the "South Side Levee" district. The area was known not only for its numerous theatres-turned-burlesque houses, but for its poolrooms, saloons, penny arcades, questionable hotels, cheap lodging houses, and "resorts." The nickel theatres and penny parlors with their barkers and flashy posters alongside burlesque houses experienced frequent police raids.

By the 1930s, burlesque shows had evolved from ensemble variety performances into simple acts of striptease. These "indecent" theatres kept the city busy, for, once they closed one, another would open in its place a short time later. Two of the popular burlesque theatres continued into the 1970s despite headlines of vulgarity.

Dime Museums and Penny Arcades

Along with vaudeville, dime museums and penny arcades also became sought-after amusements in downtown Chicago. They too were symbols of Chicago's growth after the Great Fire, along with the growing number of retail shops and department stores, hotels, office buildings, and restaurants.

The idea that the public would pay to see a collection of exotic man-made and natural curiosities became extremely popular. "Scientific oddities" like the bearded lady were featured along with mechanical curiosities and "wild" animals. Magicians, illusionists, sword swallowers, comics, banjo players, acrobats, minstrels, and dancers were all performers on the stages that were often part of the museums. Colonel J. H. Wood was the P. T. Barnum of Chicago. His first museum on Randolph Street was destroyed in the Great Fire of 1871, but Col. Wood rebuilt his museum several times. In addition to the treasures that he offered for display, he often presented a stage show with musical acts and dramas, as did the other popular amusements: Epstean's Dime Museum on Randolph Street near Clark Street, the London Dime Museum at State and Congress streets, and the Globe Museum on State near Van Buren Street.

Gradually, after 1900, the museums disappeared as the vaudeville theatres became more popular and as penny arcades opened. People no longer would pay to see the "curiosities" ("Dime Museums' Glories Dimmed," *Chicago Daily Tribune*, 18 March 1906).

Penny arcades, most often with coin-operated attractions to take your pictures or read your fortune were to be found most often on the outskirts of the central business district in storefront amusement halls. Illustrated song machines were popular in the arcades. There was a penny arcade in the heart of the Loop on State Street where the famed Orpheum stood. "The arcade was lined with metal boxes that you put a penny into and, looking through a peephole, saw action pictures of prize fighters, or pictures that were always on the verge of becoming naughty. These pictures were made by the rapid action of a book of cards, which gave the illusion of motion. As soon as you put a penny into the box a light would go on inside and you glued your eye to the peephole" ("Famed Old Orpheum Theater Will Give Way to Shoe Store," *Chicago Daily News*, 8 March 1937).

Later the arcade was remodeled, observation platforms were built into the front entrance, and travelogues staged by Hale's Tours became the place to go. You paid a dime to travel to Africa, India, or Russia. "It was just like riding a train. They even had the 'choo-choo' effect, a sound made by rubbing two pieces of sandpaper together" (www.vintagekansascity.com/halestours).

In 1907, reformers protested that the penny arcades were more in need of reform than the nickel theatres. Plainclothesmen were sent out to the South State Street "theatre district," the newspaper reported, and found "less than twenty percent of the penny moving pictures could be called decent" ("Censors Inspect Nickel Theatres," *Chicago Daily Tribune*, 1 May 1907). The Mills Edisonia Arcade at State and Van Buren Streets, the most elaborately furnished one on State Street, specialized in murder thrillers and not the "pictures that abound farther down the street." The company started as the Mills Novelty Company in 1897 and published a guide in 1907 on "how to set up a penny arcade" (www.rickcrandall.net).

2. Moving Pictures and the Nickel Theatres

As the century turned, not only did playhouses flourish, but department stores were built one after the other on State Street in the heart of the Loop. Only twenty-two years after the Chicago Fire, the city held the World's Columbian Exposition from May to October 1893. The exposition occupied 630 acres in Jackson Park along Lake Michigan and the Midway Plaisance. Daniel Burnham, the exposition's director of works, assembled an array of artistic and architectural talent to design the fair's main palatial exhibition buildings, which introduced the public to buildings of a new kind of architecture.

Penny arcades and dime museums were some of the attractions that lined the Midway Plaisance. The amusement arcades featured moving images on early, individually viewed machines like the Kinetoscope.

The Kinetoscope, or "peep-hole machine," an early moving picture exhibition device, was developed by Thomas Edison and patented in 1893. A large wooden box about four feet tall had a small viewer on the top. Inside, a film was set up on a looping system whereby the film was completely unfurled on a series of vertical rollers. Once a coin was inserted, a motor inside moved the strip of film through a revolving shutter and over a light source below the viewing device, thereby creating the illusion of movement.

Kinetoscope parlors began to appear with row upon row of these machines. Dropping a coin into a slot allowed you to look through a viewing hood for thirty seconds to see a young woman in a bathing suit or a man doing pratfalls. The Kinetoscope introduced the basic approach that would become the standard for all film projection by creating the illusion of movement.

The Mutoscope was patented by Herman Casler in 1894 and marketed by the American Mutoscope Corporation. Unlike the Kinetoscope, the Mutoscope did not rely on illumination or an electric motor and thereby gave viewers greater control over the viewing. Like the Kinetoscope, it did not project on a screen and provided viewing for one person at a time.

Later, in 1896, Edison's company purchased an improved version of the Phantascope, a movie projection machine developed by Thomas Armat. Edison renamed it the Vitascope, and it became the first commercially successful film motion picture projector in the United States.

Before the first five-cent theatre opened on State Street, there are records of moving pictures exhibited in downtown's popular playhouses. The first confirmed commercial exhibition of films in Chicago, according to the South Loop Historical Society, occurred on July 5, 1896, at the Hopkins' Theatre at 531 South State Street. The films were of New York's Herald Square, a boxing match, and concluded with *Picture of a Kiss.*

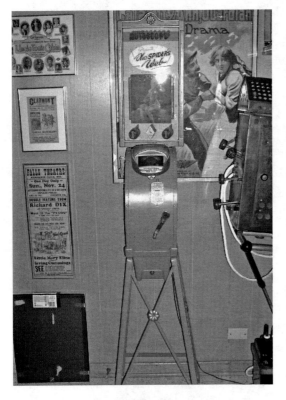

Another peep-hole machine was the Mutoscope, which worked on the same principles as a "flip-book." A sequence of photographs was arranged around the perimeter of a drum. A turn of the handle flipped the "cards" rapidly, giving the impression of movement. (Courtesy John Watson.)

On August 9, 1896, Mr. John Hopkins presented an exhibition with Edison's Vitascope at the rustic garden annex of his Hopkins' Theatre. Mr. Hopkins secured sole rights for Chicago and also reached an agreement whereby he would be informed of the latest Vitascope improvements as they became available.

"Bills at Vaudeville Houses" (*Chicago Daily Tribune*, 15 March 1897) announced that moving pictures of the president's (McKinley) inauguration could be seen at the Schiller Theatre, Hopkins' Theatre, and the Chicago Opera House. This was considered the first "newsreel."

A new apparatus for displaying moving pictures called Amet's Magniscope, a portable 35-mm film projector, was developed in 1896. The Magniscope was built by Edward Amet, in his Waukegan, Illinois Talking Machine Company. George K. Spoor, a local

Waukegan theater manager who became co-founder of Essanay Studios in Chicago helped finance the development of the projector. With the first successful commercial showing of projected moving images, many types of projectors were subsequently developed.

The Kineopticon, advertised as the best of machines to project animated pictures, was used to show President McKinley's Inaugural at Kohl and Middleton's Globe Museum on State Street on March 21, 1897.

Mr. John Hopkins brokered a deal with Veriscope to show their pictures of the Fitzsimmons-Corbett contest at his theatre and the Olympic, Clifford's Gaiety, and the Grand Opera House on June 20, 1897. All attendance records were broken at both matinee and evening performances. The new copies were taken from a new process of reproduction and proved to be clearer, with flickering reduced.

The American-Biograph pictures of the Jeffries-Sharkey contest, which took place on November 3, 1899, at Coney Island, were shown to a crowd of three hundred at the new Lyric Theatre (remodeled Gaiety) on December 2. No one noticed any strain on the eyes. The excitement from seeing moving pictures of the past Fitzsimmons-Corbett contest was forgotten.

With audiences eager to view these first magic picture shows, independent exhibitors began showing moving pictures during the summer of 1896, spurring on an increase in the production of projectors and films. Competitors of the Edison Company soon displayed their own projection systems in American theaters, including the reengineered Eidoloscope, which copied Vitascope innovations; the Lumière Cinématographe, which had already debuted in Europe in 1895; Birt Acres' Kineopticon; and the Biograph, which was marketed by the American Mutoscope Company.

The Edison Company developed its own projector known as the Projecting Kinetoscope in 1896 and abandoned marketing the Vitascope. That same year the Optigraph was introduced by A.C. Roebuck (of Sears & Roebuck) founder of the Enterprise Optical Company. In 1908 the name Optigraph was dropped when a new model was introduced under the name of Motiograph No. 1.

The American Vitagraph Company was one of the first prolific movie production companies, along with the American Mutoscope and Biograph Company (formerly the American Mutoscope Company), to record films in 1899 of a living president: William McKinley. Moving pictures soon became the starring attraction on the vaudeville bill. They made a good closing act or "chaser" for a program of vaudeville. The coming of five-cent theatres changed that pattern.

There are no records of how the first nickel theatre of 1904 in the Palmer House block on State Street was furnished, but it might have had a sheet for a screen, perhaps ten rows of folding chairs or benches, a box for collecting the nickels, and a hand-cranked projector. "Storefront theatres," the first theatres to feature the new technology of "moving pictures," were often seen in buildings that had been used for other purposes. These early silent movie theatres, at times called "nickel theatres," "five-cent theatres," or "nickelodeons," replaced the dime museums and penny arcades, attracting people to Chicago's center. Some entrepreneurs opened a nickel theatre with an adjacent arcade so there was a place to expand should the theatre become a success. So many of these early theatres opened one after the other and were only open a short time that they left no trace.

The earliest films were short in length requiring only one projector. The films were "one-reelers," a ten- to twelve-minute film, usually of 1,000 feet, the projector's reel capacity at the time. Most of the early five-cent theatres showed one-reelers using hand-cranked movie projectors. Initially, the projector's light source was a limelight, which changed to a carbon-burning arc light in the early 1900s. (Commonwealth Edison Company had been created, and downtown Chicago was connected to the electric grid.) The projector was not in an enclosed booth, and the movies were rewound on the reel by hand. The nickel theatres had no marquee but used billboards or larger posters and signs in front of the theatre to advertise the movies showing that day and to promote coming attractions. Usually the theatres changed films every day.

With the coming of larger five-cent theatres, entertainments consisted of moving pictures accompanied by illustrated songs. Haverly's Casino on Wabash was reportedly the first theatre downtown in 1895 to introduce the "song-play" or illustrated song, which was done with lantern slides. The song was "While the Dance Goes On," and the singers were Joe E. Howard and his wife. A canvas screen on the darkened stage was filled with a ballroom scene in color. As the song progressed, colored views were projected which illustrated the ballad's story. The views had been projected from hand-colored stereopticon or lantern slides made by the Chicago Transparency Company.

Nickel theatre owners and song-slide makers thrived until about 1912 when ten-cent movie theatres began to offer four- to six-reel feature films with short subjects. "Of the 250,000 sets of song slides produced between 1895 and 1913, less than 1,500 complete sets survive" (Ripley, "The Magic Lantern of Bittersweet Tears"). The early entrepreneurs began to realize that the popularity of movies wasn't fading, and theatres were built specifically to show the longer feature films and serial chapters. With the longer feature films, a second projector was installed in the booth to provide for seamless viewing from the beginning to the end of a movie.

These new theatres might have an orchestra, organ, or piano to accompany and add atmosphere to the stories unfolding on the screen. The ticket seller's booth was centered within a wide, arched entrance and exit area set back from the sidewalk, sometimes ringed by hundreds of electric lights often in a multitude of colors, some of which spelled out the name of the theatre in huge letters. The Sears Roebuck 1908 catalogue even offered a prepackaged nickelodeon front! The size and design of the theatres were shaped by preexisting and new city ordinances. Building codes and fire laws restricted seating to a maximum of 299. In addition, there were a certain number of required exists, overhead fans, low levels of lighting, and lead-lined projection booths to protect against accidents involving the highly flammable nitrate film stock.

Powers projectors and the Edison machines were the first American projectors pro-

A hand-cranked Powers Model 6 Projector with a manual-feed carbon arc lamphouse in a small downtown theatre booth, circa 1909. (Courtesy John Watson.)

duced on a commercial scale. The Powers became popular with the early small theatres. However, the open frame construction caused fire safety concerns. The Powers "Cameragraph" projectors incorporated a variation that reduced flicker on the screen. Four years later the Motiograph Model No. 1A introduced its own innovation to further reduce flicker. In between those years the Simplex projector was introduced by the Precision Machine Company and eventually came to dominate the market and be the projector of choice.

The length and number of programs in

any one theatre depended on its location. Some ran fifteen to twenty minutes in length, with forty or more shows a day if the theatre was open from morning to midnight; others ran close to an hour, much like family vaudeville, with far fewer shows. The great majority of theatres changed movies one to three times a week. The predominant moviegoers were the working-class men and women and new immigrants. The writer of a feature article (*Chicago Daily Tribune*, 26 December 1908) on "The Nickel Theatre Menace" could hardly have anticipated what was to come when he wrote, "People have become nickel theatre crazy. Chances are that the fad will run its course as others have done before it."

Film Exchanges

As the popularity of nickel theatres grew, another industry emerged in downtown Chicago. Theatre supply houses and film exchanges dotted South Wabash Avenue between Eighth and Twelfth streets. The area became known as Chicago's Film Row, the nerve center for those in the movie business, not just from Chicago but Indiana and Wisconsin. Feature films, short subjects, cartoons, lobby displays, posters, and coming attractions trailers could be had here, as well as bookings made for vaudeville acts until the "talkies" affected that amusement. National Screen Service specialized in announcement trailers. Harold Abbott's Theatre Supply sold arc lamp carbons, projectors, and screens. National Theatre offered still photos for the theatre fronts and huge billboards for outdoor displays (Teitel, "Hollywood East — Old Film Row").

Monopolized at first by the French, Chicago came to be recognized as a center for filmmaking and flourished as a film center partly because Chicago was a big theatre town that supported a steady stream of stage and vaudeville shows. Chicago enjoyed a brief reign as film capital of the world from 1907 to 1917 (Sawyers, "Way We Were").

Essanay Film Manufacturing Company and Selig Polyscope Company were two of the leading studios. William N. Selig bought one of Thomas Edison's Kinetoscopes and opened what reputedly was the country's first moving picture studio on Peck Court in 1897. Success came quickly and he built a larger studio on the northwest side. Selig's company specialized in "jungle" and travel films, with the Indiana Dunes substituting for the Sahara Desert. Essanay Studios was formed in 1907 by George K. Spoor and Gilbert A. Anderson. Mr. Anderson was "Bronco Billy," the first western "movie star," who had appeared in *The Great Train Robbery*, the first narrative western film that told a story. Essanay concentrated on slapstick and light domestic comedies with comedian Ben Turpin. Essanay Films made the city a moviemaking center. Four out of every five U.S. movies were produced in Chicago until 1913 when Essanay Films moved to California (Loerzel, "Reel Chicago").

The movie studios were created to make the constant supply of films needed for the moving picture machines. This was especially true in the days of one-reel presentations. During this period, the movies that were made were little more than "staged theatre." Later, multiple feature-length films were needed to assure rotation and a constant new supply for the new larger theatres.

Even while the excitement of the new moving pictures grew in Chicago, the older playhouses continued their popularity, especially the McVicker's, Auditorium, Studebaker, Apollo, Garrick, Great Northern, and Powers' theatres, and the Grand Opera House. New theatres were built during the first years of the new century: namely, the Illinois, LaSalle, Iroquois, and Majestic.

Fire struck the new Iroquois Theatre only five weeks after it opened on December 30, 1903. A painted canvas piece of scenery above the stage too close to a spotlight caught fire during a matinee performance with a standing-room-only crowd of almost 1,900. That piece fell to the stage, the asbestos cur-

Clark Street in 1928 with two popular playhouses, the Grand Opera House, which would eventually show movies as the RKO Grand, and the Erlanger, a very popular playhouse that opened as the Palace Music Hall.

tain malfunctioned, and combustible items ignited instantly. Those on stage rushed out the stage door letting in a blast of air, which only fed the fire more, causing it to jump into the auditorium and then the balconies. It was the deadliest blaze in Chicago history with 602 casualties far surpassing the 250 that had died in the Great Chicago Fire of 1871 (Brandt, Duis, and Schallhorn, *Chicago Death Trap*).

So it was not surprising to read in the *Chicago Daily Tribune* of January 5, 1904: "Theatres Closed for a Fortnight; Some Houses Must Rebuild and All Are Advised to

Await Council Action." Mayor Harrison informed a delegation of playhouse managers that not a single place of amusement would be allowed to open until every detail of the law had been complied with. The changes ranged from securing fireproof curtains to actual reconstruction of the buildings. Foremost was the requirement that theatre doors open outwards. The magnitude of the Iroquois disaster had shaken the foundation of the building ordinances. The Grand Opera House and Powers' Theatre were built before city ordinances required fireproof construction. The Olympic did not have an asbestos curtain; the Garrick Theatre faced only two open sides instead of the three open sides required by city ordinance; and the Auditorium, Illinois, McVicker's, Cleveland's, and Studebaker theatres had no automatic sprinklers. Later that month, several houses announced that they were closing because of the estimated cost of meeting the new theatre ordinances. One such theatre was Steinway Hall, which was later reconstructed and opened as the Whitney Opera House. By October of that year, Cleveland's advertised "Greater Vaudeville in the Only Safest Theatre, Matinee Daily," and the McVicker's called itself "the safest theatre in the world."

The number of playhouses in downtown Chicago was imposing, and people considered the city a theatrical center second to none by 1910. Chicago's Rialto (theatre district), the *Chicago Daily Tribune* (13 October 1907) wrote, would one day rival New York's: "Chicago's theatre district extended (in the first decade of the century) from the northeast corner of Randolph and Clark streets as far west as the Powers' Theatre and as far east as the Colonial passing the Garrick and the Olympic theatres. The little stretch of Washington Street from the Chicago Opera House to Clark Street, Clark Street from Washington to Randolph, and Randolph Street from the Powers' to the Colonial theatres."

So imposing was the list of playhouses that they began to specialize in the type of

entertainments they offered: the McVicker's, Great Northern, Globe, and Grand Opera House were home to dramas; comedy held stage at the Chicago Opera House, Garrick, Powers,' Illinois, and Studebaker theatres; the Majestic and Olympic theatres usually featured vaudeville; the Whitney Opera House, American Music Hall, LaSalle, Playhouse, Princess, Ziegfeld, and Colonial theatres all presented lighter musical plays; the small Cort theatre featured domestic comedies; and the Auditorium was home to opera and concerts. Theatregoers of the time had their choice of productions of every description.

Over time the nickel theatres became outdated. Larger, better-equipped photoplay houses were built with the development of feature films such as D. W. Griffith's twelve-reel *Birth of a Nation* in 1915. This epic film, considered by film historians as one of the first feature-length American films, lasted a little over three hours. Extremely controversial in content, the movie did introduce new cross-cutting and editing techniques.

Existing legitimate theatres (the Orpheum, for example) were turned into moving picture theatres with admission costing ten and fifteen cents. Around the end of the first decade and into the next, advancements in plaster and terra cotta allowed the owners of new moving picture theatres to provide more ornament in their buildings. For example, pressed tin ceilings became a feature in some theatres.

Early entrepreneurs such as Aaron Jones teamed with Adolph Linick and Peter Schaefer to form one of the earliest theatre circuits. These men realized that the popularity of movies wasn't going to fade because of the success of the many nickel theatres that had opened. Larger photoplay theatres began to appear in the Loop, or existing legitimate theatres were turned into moving picture houses. In an article entitled "Chicago's Picture Prosperity" in the January 17, 1916, issue of *Variety*, the writer concluded that moving picture theatres were here to stay! The "movie kings," as Jones, Linick and Schaefer were called, had started with a single nickel theatre on State Street that grew into Chicago's first chain of film theatres, numbering fifty-two at one time. They became known as one of the first Chicago theatre chains and one of the largest.

Jones, Linick and Schaefer

In 1904, Mr. Jones of the firm Jones, Linick and Schaefer started the first nickel theatre in downtown Chicago on State Street in the Palmer House block near Adams Street. Previously a store, it was the first theatre to put on a complete moving picture show. That success proved to be the impetus for the phenomenal growth of the Jones, Linick and Schaefer firm. When the lease to that first storefront theatre could not be extended, an arcade directly across the street was rented, which was turned into another picture show in 1906 called Hale's Tours of the World. The exterior represented the rear end of two Pullman train cars. Called an "illusion ride," the moving pictures depicted scenes from around the world making it seem as if you were seated on an actual train. The possibilities of this new form of entertainment were realized with this success.

It was on this site that the firm built the Orpheum in 1907 with a seating capacity of 799. Theatre managers in Chicago were shocked to see the big electric peacock over the entrance, which was a bad omen among theatre people. Instead, the Orpheum had great fortune, breaking all attendance records among the downtown amusements.

That same year, Jones, Linick and Schaefer opened the Bijou Dream next door to the Orpheum. This theatre presented vaudeville and penny arcade entertainment, with a dime museum on the second floor. Within two years it was devoted to pictures and illustrated songs. On the second floor, photoplays could be seen for five cents, while downstairs a vaudeville show cost ten cents. By 1915 it would be the home of feature pictures and hold the record of the longest run on State Street of any film shown in Chicago.

From 1908 to 1909, Jones, Linick and Schaefer built or leased the Lyric, Premier, Gem, Unique, National, American, and Comique theatres on State Street. The Lyric was the only theatre in the world that stayed open day and night. The manager asserted that the lights had never been out, the doors had never closed, and the projection had never stopped. The Premier featured vaudeville and pictures, as did the Gem. The Gem used one reel of 1,000 feet of film per week while presenting six acts of vaudeville divided into two shifts. The Unique Theatre just showed moving pictures from Essanay, Selig, Gaumont, Pathe, and Edison. On Madison Street, the Alcazar, Rose, and Star theatres were also acquired by Jones, Linick and Schaefer.

The area on Madison Street between South Clark and Dearborn streets was now dubbed "Picture Row" because of the cluster of smaller moving picture houses within that block. The number of moving picture theatres would only continue to grow.

All the theatres opened by the firm were equipped with up-to-date projection equipment and deluxe seats. The ornamental plasterwork and lighting fixtures were furnished by Decorators Supply Company.

The Colonial Theatre in the heart of the Rialto, devoted to musical comedy and legitimate drama, was acquired by Jones, Linick and Schaefer on May 9, 1913, to the surprise of the downtown theatre world. "10–15–25" cent vaudeville was featured.

Six weeks later the firm announced that the McVicker's Theatre had been acquired and would be devoted to vaudeville and pictures. Immediately following that, a lease was closed for the Studebaker Theatre. Traditions of long standing had been shattered.

Another legitimate theatre that had gained renown as the birthplace of musical comedy, the LaSalle Theatre, was leased on December 10, 1913. *September Morn*, a musical comedy, was permitted to continue its

Madison Street in 1926 shows the Rose Theatre and three doors down the Alcazar Theatre with banners and posters covering more than half the theatre's entrance.

run. By 1916 it was given over to the exhibition of motion pictures.

Jones, Linick and Schaefer advertised the first moving pictures at the Studebaker Theatre on November 14, 1914. *On Belgian Battlefields in the Great European War* was advertised as the first authentic motion picture of the war. The four reels of actual fighting were shot by Edwin F. Weigle, staff war photographer for the *Chicago Tribune*. When moving pictures failed to bring in a profit, the Shubert and Erlanger organization reopened the Studebaker on November 5, 1917, as a legitimate theatre.

The Colonial Theatre had been the first to present *The German Side of the War* on July 22, 1916. The six reels were also the work of Edwin F. Weigle for the *Chicago Tribune*. In response to America's entry into World War I in April 1917, *Joan the Woman* was presented at the Colonial.

The year 1917 found Jones, Linick and Schaefer the leading film exhibitors in the Loop. They had just opened the Rialto Theatre on South State Street with vaudeville and photoplays, and the following year, at the other end of State Street, they opened the Randolph Theatre on Christmas Day for showing movies only. The Randolph was one of the earliest and largest Loop movie houses without a stage.

In 1922, Jones, Linick and Schaefer had the (third) McVicker's razed to build a "movie palace" on the site of the older theatre. Having acquired the exclusive Paramount Studios' franchise for Chicago, they announced that their new McVickers would show only Paramount films beginning with the opening show. It was then that the circuit moved their corporate offices to the McVicker's Building from the Rialto Theatre Building. The McVickers, like the Rialto, also presented "high-class, popular price" vaudeville. At the same time, their Randolph Theatre had been leased by Universal, and the Bijou Dream closed. In 1923, the Woods Theatre came under the management of Jones, Linick and Schaefer and featured first-run pictures.

The twentieth anniversary of the theatre circuit in 1924 was celebrated at the Orpheum with Harold Lloyd in his latest, "first time shown anywhere" comedy feature *Hot Water*. The Rialto Theatre also featured an anniversary show.

The acquisition of the State-Lake Theatre marked a milestone for Jones, Linick and Schaefer. It was their fiftieth theatre. (They also owned theatres in Chicago's neighborhoods, downstate Illinois, Indiana, and Wisconsin.) Their management began on July 23, 1933, with vaudeville and exclusive photoplays. On March 15, 1934, they leased the Majestic, with Aaron Jones managing the playhouse. A combination of movies and vaudeville became the new policy.

Jones, Linick and Schaefer really were the "movie kings" of the city, living up to their motto: "First In Amusements, in Price, in the Hearts of Chicago Playgoers."

The reviews and listings of downtown amusements in the *Chicago Daily Tribune* throughout the second decade listed both a schedule of dramas and comedies at the popular playhouses, such as the Colonial, Powers, Cort, Illinois, Cohan's Grand, Princess, Garrick, and Playhouse, interspersed with reviews of current feature films. Six more downtown playhouses had been built to grow the list of theatres: Blackstone (1910), Columbia (1911), Palace Music Hall (1912), Rialto (1917), Woods (1918) and State-Lake (1919).

Vaudeville was featured at the Palace

Music Hall and Majestic, and in 1913 moving pictures of Fred and Irene Castle dancing were added to the program. In addition, on February 20, 1913, Thomas A. Edison was the "headliner" in both theatres. Moving pictures had the place of honor on the bill. Mr. Edison presented his "kinetophone," which was described as the "synchronization of reproduced sound and sight."

One critic described it as the Victrola and camera in perfect combination, concluding it was a wonderful apparatus. Mr. Edison's company also gave us the first American serial film in 1912, a melodrama called *What Happened to Mary?* with twelve episodes, each one reel. By 1914, serials regularly added cliffhangers as one of their features, notably *The Perils of Pauline* in twenty episodes. Captive audiences would watch Pearl White bound to the rails hoping she would escape the onrushing train.

The Princess added the movie *Quo Vadis* to its variety program and presented the drama *Uncle Tom's Cabin* in 1914. The Studebaker advertised the first moving pictures taken on the front lines during WWI and also featured a Victor Herbert operetta that same season. The LaSalle featured the popular Essanay six-reeler *The Blindness of Virtue*. The Vitagraph production of *The Battle Cry of Peace* could be seen at the Olympic in 1915. Before the next decade, in 1918, the Auditorium presented the patriotic film *The Unbeliever*, and the Ziegfeld Theatre screened a Douglas Fairbanks film. On the first Armistice Day, November 11, 1918, the Palace Music Hall played two-a-day vaudeville: the Great Northern, Majestic, Rialto, and McVicker's also featured vaudeville, with a Charlie Chaplin film added to the bill at the Rialto and McVicker's. The Chicago Opera Company was performing at the Auditorium.

The next decade would see movie theatres built downtown to resemble grand palaces with over one thousand seats. One of those would become the symbol of Chicago.

3. The Movie Palaces and the Films That Talked

Chicagoans were going to the show in record numbers during the twenties and early thirties. "People went downtown to be entertained" (Valentine, *The Show Starts on the Sidewalk*). This was the era a record number of "grand, awe-inspiring edifices" were built called movie palaces, some referred to as the golden age of movie houses. The theatre setting was sumptuous enough to evoke a dreamy atmosphere and allow the audience to forget, for the evening, the ordinary world that remained outside the doors. Ben Hall, movie historian, so rightly described the movie palace as "an acre of seats in a garden of dreams."

Throughout the 1920s, extravagant opulence might be the words used to describe the grand movie palaces built in downtown Chicago. These picture palaces borrowed from past French, Italian, Spanish, and Moorish architecture. Many were designed as replicas of Old World palaces and churches. Their huge domed auditoriums were decorated with ornate columns, marble and gold statues, ceiling friezes, great crystal chandeliers, sweeping staircases, and pools with fountains. Painted or gilt plaster in intricate ornamented patterns was applied to ceilings, walls, and columns. Silk and velvet fabrics were used for drapes and the upholstery of overstuffed chairs. Some interiors evoked a night sky with twinkling stars. These movie palaces offered a respite from the real world.

Movie theatres spoiled patrons with services and luxurious extras such as nurseries and playrooms, and uniformed ushers in elaborate uniforms were also on hand. There were restrooms with personal attendants and smoking lounges.

The Chicago, called "the Wonder Theatre of the World," was the flagship of the Balaban and Katz theatre chain. Its large vertical sign was to become not only a symbol of State Street, but of the city itself. The Chicago Theatre is considered the first "motion picture palace" in the nation, and the oldest survivor in Chicago. It set the standard and started the explosion of extravagant picture palaces nationwide.

Five years later, C. W. Rapp and George L. Rapp designed the Oriental and Palace theatres. Often inspired by French architecture, their theatres were excesses of extravagance, filled with giant crystal chandeliers, walls and floors made of Italian marble, gold plaster ornamentation, majestic staircases, fountains and pools that sometimes even had swans. The theatres were large enough to seat from three to four thousand people, and their enormous vertical signs and marquees were lit by hundreds of lights and colored neon. Some of their theatres still remain today in downtown Chicago: the Chicago, Oriental, and Palace theatres have been converted into centers for the performing arts.

The Chicago season of 1922–1923 that

The first picture palace built in the Loop was the Chicago Theater in 1921 designed by the most renowned movie theater architects of the time, C. W. Rapp and George L. Rapp.

began on Labor Day (and ended June 30) played more than one hundred theatre attractions in twenty-two playhouses, including the Harris and Selwyn theatres, which both opened in 1922.

With the arrival of the palatial theatres and the greater seating capacity that these theatres possessed, movie attendance doubled, competing with the legitimate theatres to attract audiences: Auditorium, Civic, Garrick, Studebaker, Cohan's Grand, Cort, Olympic, Woods, Illinois, Colonial, Powers, Great Northern, Princess, Apollo, LaSalle, Erlanger, Blackstone, Central, McVicker's, and Majestic theatres. Along with the Harris and Selwyn Theatres, these were the major theatres downtown during this time. The next decade would see that number greatly diminish.

In the fall of 1925, another "attraction" was put in place for downtown theatregoers: a "Canyon of Light" ("State Street to Be Made Canyon of Light," *Chicago Daily Tribune*, 27 August 1925). The electric illumination of State Street would turn it into a "dazzling canyon of light, two and a half times brighter than any other thoroughfare in America." Ornate metal posts, each bearing two 4,000 candlepower lamps, were placed at intervals of one hundred feet on each side of State Street from Van Buren to Lake streets. Twenty lamps were located in each block lighted from dusk until 1:00 A.M. "No other city in the country will have the 'bright lights' to compare with Chicago," said an engineer of the Edison Company. All the major department stores on State Street, including Marshall Field and Company, and the Roosevelt Theatre across its State Street entrance, promoted the plan. Electricity helped make State Street a profitable retail and entertainment zone by attracting Chicagoans to the area well after dark, long after the business day was done.

By the end of the 1920s, there were no less than three department stores, seven movie palaces, and dozens of restaurants and nightclubs within two blocks of the intersection of State and Randolph. Streetcars ran along State Street and throughout the city. The fare was seven cents. In 1927 gasoline-powered buses began to appear, eventually making the streetcar obsolete.

The perfection of sound synchronized to film movement eventually brought an end to the silent movie era in the late twenties. Even though the silents had given us many memorable movies, there were limitations in storytelling. This led to the development of two competing sound or recording systems: *sound optically printed on film* and *sound-on-disc*.

The first approach was demonstrated on a short-subject film in 1923 at the Rivoli Theatre in New York City by Lee DeForest's Phonofilm system using components by Theodore Case and his colleague Earl Sponable. A falling-out with DeForest prompted Case and Sponable in 1926 to demonstrate their system to William Fox of Fox Film Corporation. Impressed, Fox went into partnership with Case, creating the Fox-Case Corporation to commercialize sound film. Developed in conjunction with General Electric Company, the new system was called Movietone, with the slogan "It speaks for itself." When Fox became the first motion picture studio to record sound-on-film, the Movietone News Service resulted.

In 1925, the Vitaphone Company (a subsidiary created by Warner Bros. and Western Electric Corporation) developed the second approach of sound-on-disc. In essence, the sound was contained on a sixteen-inch record running at 33.3 rpm that was synchronized with the projector. The first feature-length film with synchronized Vitaphone sound effects and musical soundtrack, without spoken dialogue, was the Warner Bros. 1926 swashbuckler film *Don Juan* starring John Barrymore. The movie launched a serious attempt to win support for a wholesale changeover to sound. *Don Juan* premiered at the Orpheum on February 18, 1927.

Sunrise, directed by F. W. Murnau, was the first feature with a soundtrack of music and sound effects recorded in the Fox Movietone sound-on-film system. The film was released on September 23, 1927, and, as with *Don Juan*, the film's soundtrack consisted of a musical score and sound effects. The first sound news film released by Fox-Movietone News was of Charles Lindbergh's takeoff on May 20, 1927, from New York for his flight across the Atlantic to Paris.

State Street in the mid–1920s looking south from Randolph Street. One of Marshall Field's clocks can be seen in the lower left-hand corner. Installed in 1897, Field's clock became the place to meet downtown.

Earl Sponable's development of a porous screen in 1927 allowed speakers behind the screen instead of below or to the side of the screen as in the first theatre speakers. This center placement became the standard until the wide-screen processes of the 1950s.

The Jazz Singer starring Al Jolson was released on October 6, 1927, by Warner Bros. The film's box office success was attributed largely to Al Jolson, one of America's biggest musical stars. The movie had a synchronized musical score and sound effects using Vitaphone's system. *The Jazz Singer* was the first feature-length Hollywood film in which spoken dialogue was used in a part of the dramatic action. *The Jazz Singer* premiered on November 29, 1927, at the Garrick Theatre.

The first "all-talking" (or all-dialogue) feature-length movie was Warner Bros. gangster film *Lights of New York* released July 6, 1928, directed by Bryan Foy. It was the first film to define the crime genre. Sound films were so enthusiastically received that Hollywood was producing sound films exclusively by 1929. *Lights of New York* premiered at the McVickers Theatre on August 3, 1928.

In 1928, Disney released their first animated sound film, *Steamboat Willie*, starring Mickey Mouse. The short was made with a fully synchronized soundtrack of music, sound effects, and dialogue, recorded optically as sound-on-film.

The first of MGM's "all-talking, all-singing, and all-dancing" films, *The Broad-*

way Melody, premiered on February 1, 1929, after the studio licensed the sound-on-film process. The first sound film to win an Academy Award for Best Picture, the film was one of the first musicals to feature a Technicolor sequence.

The motion picture soundtrack was standardized as a single track printed optically on the edge of the film in 1930. The sound-on-disc system was considered to be too costly and presented long-term issues in tracking the disc with the film distribution.

Movie studios, realizing their future was in "the new movies that talked," began building the appropriate studios. Some established stars of the silent screen disappeared from the moviemaking business because their voices were not acceptable (as portrayed in the movie *Singing in the Rain*) for one reason or another. Some smaller theatres would eventually close their doors because of the cost of installing either the sound-on-disc or sound-on-film equipment.

Balaban & Katz were the predominant theatre men in Chicago from the 1920s until World War II ended and were responsible for the major movie palaces in downtown Chicago.

Balaban and Katz

Barney and A. J. Balaban opened their first nickelodeon on Chicago's West Side in 1908 and then built the Circle Theatre, the first Chicago movie house with a balcony. The Balabans and Sam Katz next opened the Central Park, the first theatre with modern air conditioning. In 1917 they formed the Balaban and Katz Theatre Corporation, which included brothers A. J., Barney, John, and Max Balaban with their friends Sam and Morris Katz. In 1925 Balaban and Katz Corporation merged with Famous Players-Lasky (Paramount Pictures) resulting in the Publix Theatre chain. They now had access to Hollywood's top films. That same year they purchased seventeen Lubliner and Trinz movie theatres. More than five hundred theatres in the country were brought under one management.

By the mid–1930s, sixty-five million Americans went to movie houses each week, despite the Depression. Balaban and Katz theatres not only showed first-run movies but also hosted star performers on the large stages of their movie palaces. "In Balaban and Katz palaces, the moviegoer was royalty" (Balaban, *The Chicago Movie Palaces of Balaban and Katz*). White-gloved ushers escorted patrons to their seats. Service to the patron was important to the theatre chain. Free child care, attendant smoking rooms, playgrounds with nurses and attendants, and afternoon tea shows for women were promoted in their theatres.

Most movie houses in the Midwest simply closed during the summer. Balaban and Katz theatres were the first mechanically air-cooled theatres in the world, and with the Chicago, the first theatre to add a dehumidifier. For several years their theatres were the only air-conditioned theatres in Chicago. "Relax, Refresh, Revitalize" became their motto.

Balaban and Katz also worked to develop a family-oriented image, referring to their movie palaces in advertisements as "delightful vacation spots for the youngsters." A free weekly magazine, in color, was distributed to customers to promote upcoming "best pictures" and stage shows in all their theatres.

Theatre architecture reached a level never seen before: a fantasy world of gold and bronze, crystal chandeliers, grand lobbies as big as the auditoriums, and galleries lined with paintings and sculpture. Outside vertical signs as tall as buildings were lit night and day to announce the theatre. Their "continuous performance" philosophy meant that the theatres opened in the morning and played through the night, showing movies, short subjects or newsreels, live shows, and musical stage productions, such as jazz bands, house orchestras, and dance revues. During

The 1938 banner on the Roosevelt Theatre not only echoed the Balaban and Katz philosophy, but offered the chance of winning money to draw patrons into their theatres.

the 1920s, the price of admission was thirty cents during the day and fifty cents in the evening. Live shows changed once a week.

The Chicago Theatre was their first theatre in downtown Chicago built in 1921, designed by C. W. and George L. Rapp. This was the first opulent movie palace in the country and became the model for all others. Called "the Wonder Theatre of the World," it became the flagship of the Balaban and Katz theatre chain. On the facade, a large circular stained-glass panel bore the coat of arms of the Balaban and Katz chain: two horses holding ribbons of 35-mm film in their mouths. The auditorium was seven stories high, more than one half of a city block wide, and nearly as long. The vertical sign "C-H-I-C-A-G-O," at six stories high, is one of the few such signs in existence today. A symbol of State Street and the city itself, the sign and marquee became landmarks in themselves. On the seventh floor of the

Chicago Theatre building was the "Little Chicago Theatre" or Balaban and Katz's "screening room." Every feature picture and every short subject was previewed and judged to obtain the best pictures (*Chicago Daily Tribune*, 31 July 1936).

Balaban and Katz purchased the Roosevelt Theatre from the Ascher Brothers in 1922. It was considered the Loop's finest movie house until the Chicago Theatre was built. This was their fifth house, and A. J. Balaban personally operated the theatre. A Kimball theatre organ had been installed in the theatre, but live stage shows were not presented. Instead, on June 26, 1936, the Joe Louis-Max Schmeling fight pictures were booked as an extra screen attraction.

Designed by C. W. Rapp and George L. Rapp for Balaban and Katz in 1926, the Oriental is in the rear portion occupying floors one through eight of the twenty-three story New United Masonic Temple building. This

was their most colorful and picturesque theatre, one that would "charm away workaday worries and make it easy for audiences to forget everything but the entertainment before them." The exotic Oriental Theatre presented first-run films and lavish stage shows hosted by Paul Ash and his "Merry Mad Musical Gang." It earned a reputation as one of the city's best places to enjoy live performances.

In 1926, Balaban and Katz also acquired the McVickers Theatre. The McVickers would have the distinction of premiering the first all-talking feature film *Lights of New York*.

The interior of the United Artists Theatre was redesigned for a film audience by C. Howard Crane in an eclectic mix of Spanish, Moorish, and Middle Eastern styles. The theatre was the debut venue in Chicago for all major United Artists releases. Balaban and Katz acquired the United Artists in 1929 continuing the theatre as a moving picture theatre without vaudeville or other attractions.

The Publix-Balaban and Katz theatre chain purchased the Garrick in 1934 and converted it into a movie theatre. A. M. Strauss was responsible for the remodel that used aluminum and Vitrolite to "modernize" what was felt to be an antiquated front. Not only did this clash with Adler and Sullivan's original design, but the new, larger marquee that was erected obscured Sullivan's original terra cotta decoration.

In 1934, Balaban and Katz also leased the Apollo, extensively remodeling the theatre to reopen the Apollo as a movie house. An air-conditioning plant was installed as had been done in the neighboring Garrick Theatre. Converting the Apollo to a motion picture theatre meant that the last home of legitimate drama on Randolph Street, on the old "Rialto," was gone.

The State-Lake was acquired by Bala-ban and Katz on November 6, 1936, but their management of the theatre would not begin until May 1, 1937, as Jones, Linick and Schaefer had the lease until then. Across the street from the Chicago Theatre, C. W. Rapp and George L. Rapp designed the theatre in a French Renaissance style. During the late 1930s, the State-Lake was one of the film houses that presented stage shows or vaudeville acts along with feature films.

During the 1930s, "Balaban and Katz Wonder Theatres" headed their movie listings in the *Chicago Tribune*, and despite movie attendance reflecting the general business decline, B&K theatres continued to prosper. In 1931 a "movies-only" policy was ordered by Paramount, signaling the end of live shows. Theatres wishing to stay in business during the Depression cut their budgets. Moviegoers no longer expected some of the amenities offered by the movie palaces. Balaban and Katz advertised six "Wonder Theatres" in the Loop: the Chicago, Roosevelt, State-Lake, United Artists, Garrick, and Apollo. In the projection booths of their theatres were Brenkert Model BX80 projectors with RCA soundheads, and Brenkert Enarc carbon arc lamps.

In 1939 Balaban and Katz founded the first commercial television station, WBKB, in Chicago. John Balaban, who headed the station, allowed the U.S. government to use the facility for training purposes during World War II. WBKB was first housed in the State-Lake building and later moved, in 1950, to the Garrick Theatre. At that time Balaban and Katz began to realize the potential of television as a sales and promotional tool. Movie trailers and a weekly variety show were planned to highlight their show-biz history (*Billboard*, 27 August 1949).

After the successful premier in January 1953 of *Bwana Devil*, the first 3-D film shown in Chicago, President John Balaban

Opposite top: Air-conditioning equipment for motion picture houses revolutionized summer patronage. B&K's publicity reminded Chicago of the treat here in this 1937 banner. *Opposite bottom:* Roosevelt Theatre in 1937 displayed "A World of Happiness for Everyone" banner.

The Woods Theatre on Randolph Street in 1936 with the large vertical sign of the United Artists Theatre on the opposite corner. The vertical sign of the Oriental Theatre can be seen in the distance.

announced three months later that the Chicago Theatre would feature Warner's new 3-D film, *House of Wax*. The use of special glasses was required to view the films (Tinee, "Theater Man Reports on the New 3-D Films").

Balaban and Katz had operated under their name for fifty years, but on June 5, 1968, the firm was renamed ABC-Great States Inc. The change was made to identify the company more closely with its parent organization, American Broadcasting Companies Inc.

In 1930, Ray Bolger was on stage at the Chicago bringing in large audiences, and Helen Kane, the Boop-a-Doop Girl, held the stage at the Oriental. The Palace and State-Lake theatres were "Radio-Keith-Orpheum Cool." The Woods presented the "all-talking, all-singing" picture of the year, Pathe picture *Swing High* plus Pathe news and a "riotous comedy." The Punch and Judy featured the "first all-talking German drama with music."

The first season of 1930 still counted over twenty playhouses, but with a shrunken list of playbills: Adelphi, Apollo, Auditorium, Blackstone, Cort, Civic, Erlanger, Garrick, Four Cohans, Great Northern, Harris, Majestic, Princess, Selwyn, and Studebaker theatres.

The Blackstone and Great Northern theatres had been reopened by WPA programs, and the Cort, which had reopened in 1931, would close its doors just three years later.

The Adelphi became the most unique movie theatre in Chicago. Renamed the Clark in 1933, the theatre showed a different double feature every day of the year. In 1934, the Illinois and Majestic theatres would close their doors while the Garrick and Apollo theatres began showing moving pictures, now operated by Balaban and Katz.

In 1939, the "all-talking" moving picture had become the amusement of choice, leaving only four playhouses that had not become movie houses. The Depression had also contributed to the closure of many playhouses and eventually put a stop to the building of enormous theatres. Only one new motion picture theatre was built downtown after the Depression. With people eager to hear news of the war, the Telenews Theatre opened in 1939 on State Street next to the Chicago Theatre.

4. An Era Ends

When World War II started, "news-hungry" people attended the movies for the latest reports of the war. Newsreels accompanied the feature films in the downtown theatres. Theatres supported the war effort with bond drives while the studios released movies with patriotic themes that helped keep up the spirit of the public.

Two small movie theatres downtown, the Today and Telenews, continuously ran newsreels; the Telenews Theatre, the last theatre to be built downtown, allowed patrons to get up-to-the-minute reports from the front with an operating United Press Teletype in the lobby.

A decade later, theatre attendance dropped by half. The 1930s and some of the 1940s had been labeled "the Golden Age of Hollywood." Sound had been developed and advanced; color had been introduced. New film genres emerged as well, such as musicals, gangster films, westerns, and comedies.

Also during the early 1940s large portions of State Street were torn up for the building of its subway and the relocation of underground utilities. Opening of the subway with separate entries into ten buildings set the stage in 1943 for the post-war improvement programs, which made State Street shopping a more enjoyable experience. Every department store from one end to the other was modernized. The State Street Council was formed to maintain the prestige of the famous street. In addition to the large department stores, there were specialty shops, drug stores, and eateries like Hardings and Toffenetti's, now replaced with McDonald's and Starbucks. State Street became the shopping center for the city. The prime meeting place was under Marshall Field's clock at State and Washington streets.

When the Shubert (formerly Majestic) Theatre reopened in the mid–1940s, only a total of nine playhouses were open downtown: Blackstone, Great Northern, Harris, Selwyn, Studebaker, Erlanger, and Civic theatres. Shakespeare was being performed at the Auditorium. The Civic Opera House was usually devoted to opera, ballet, and concerts. In the 1946–1947 season, the Civic Theatre featured twenty-two weeks of the Technicolor English film *Henry V* with Laurence Olivier. The number of shows each season began to decrease as the 1950s neared. The Great Northern was closed because of new fire laws, resulting from the LaSalle Hotel fire disaster of 1946. A raging fire swept through much of the hotel on June 5 claiming the lives of sixty-one persons, including children. Most of the persons died from asphyxiation when they opened their hotel room doors and their rooms filled with thick smoke. (The LaSalle Hotel was built in 1909 at the corner of LaSalle and Madison streets.) There were reports of extensive remodeling, but at season's end (June 1947), the Great Northern was still dark.

By contrast one could see a first-run film and stage show in any of nine picture palaces: the Chicago, Oriental, State-Lake, Roo-

Looking west down Randolph Street from under Marshall Field's clock on State Street.

sevelt, McVickers, Woods, United Artists, Garrick, Palace, and Grand theatres. The latest news could be seen at the Today and Telenews theatres. The Clark Theatre ran a double feature that changed daily plus the "Latest News." The Roosevelt was featuring the film *Best Years of Our Lives*, winner of nine Academy Awards. Following the end of the war, Hollywood's most profitable year in the decade was 1946, with all-time highs recorded for theatre attendance.

Serials were usually found in neighborhood theatres, so it was a surprise to find the Palace Theatre in August 1948 advertising Disney's *Melody Time* and chapter 3 of *Superman*.

Ruth Gordon, noted stage actress, wrote in Claudia Cassidy's column in the *Chicago*

Tribune in September 1948, "Where did they all get lost?" referring to the Princess, Cort, LaSalle, Cohan's Grand, Powers,' and Illinois theatres. "Hang on," she wrote to the Erlanger, Studebaker, Blackstone, Shubert, Great Northern, Civic, Harris, and Selwyn. The Harris and Selwyn theatres, referred to as the "twin temples of the seven arts of the stage," were the last legitimate theatres built in downtown Chicago, ("Chicago-Midwest 1986 Conclave," *Marquee*, 1986.)

However, as people began to learn of the new medium of television, newsreels became a thing of the past. People could get news broadcasts without leaving home. At the same time the major department stores on State Street began to lose large numbers of customers with people moving to the suburbs. "A car in every driveway and a television in every living room" seemed to be our pursuit after the war. As suburbia expanded, the newly built suburban shopping malls gave birth to the multiplex: narrow, small, characterless theatres, many under one roof, necessitated by efficient operation and cost. Downtown movie theatres, like major department stores and hotels, began their downward decline.

In the early 1950s, Hollywood began to react to competition from the small black-and-white screen television sets now in almost everyone's living room. In an effort to entice people back downtown, theatre audiences were introduced to films in color on large screens with new technical processes called 3-D, Cinerama, CinemaScope, Todd-AO, and VistaVision. By the mid–50s more than half of Hollywood's productions were made in color.

The 3-D films of the 1950s were photographed by two cameras, one representing each eye, and were shown by two projection machines throwing one picture on top of the other on the screen. The two reels projected at once had to be kept in perfect synchronization by the projectionist. Special polarized cardboard glasses had to be worn by theatregoers to coordinate the images, making the action seem to jump off the screen. The glasses were not popular, and the 3-D effects were not enough to compensate for the inferior quality of most of the films. The first full-length, 3-D feature sound film was the 1952 United Artists jungle adventure, *Bwana Devil*. Its taglines advertised "A Lion in Your Lap." The film premiered at the Chicago Theatre on January 23, 1953 ("First Feature Stereo Movie to Open Today," *Chicago Tribune*, 23 January 1953).

Cinerama was a widescreen process, which worked by simultaneously projecting three separate camera images (left, center, and right views of a subject) from three synchronized 35-mm projectors onto a large, deeply curved screen with four-track stereo sound. Three projection booths were required. The impression of depth and reality achieved with Cinerama was an experience unlike any other without putting on special glasses. Cinerama became a theatrical event complete with reserved seating and printed programs.

The Palace Theatre became the Chicago home of Cinerama with the first showing of *This Is Cinerama* in 1953. The new, curved screen extended from the orchestra pit to the ceiling of the large stage. It was the largest screen ever used in a movie house. When Cinerama celebrated its fourth birthday at the Palace, the *Chicago Tribune* (28 July 1957) reported that it was the longest run of any movie attraction in the history of Chicago. The fad ended in 1959 with the fifth Cinerama film, *South Seas Adventure*.

A widescreen, single-camera process was introduced by Twentieth Century-Fox called CinemaScope. A special anamorphic lens that photographed motion pictures with an ordinary camera was required. Basically, an anamorphic lens is a lens that optically distorts the image. It was first developed in the film industry as a way to use standard 35mm film to record images in widescreen format. By fitting the film camera with a widescreen format lens, the image could be optically compressed so that it would fit into a 35mm film frame. Then when the film was played through a

In 1949, despite the visible changes looking east on Randolph Street, the Woods Theatre appears nearly unchanged. The large vertical signs of the United Artists and Oriental theatres are not to be seen.

projection system, the projector was fitted with another lens that reversed the distortion. In this way the compressed image that was recorded on the 35mm film was projected onto the screen in a natural, uncompressed widescreen format.

The theatre owner had to widen his screen, which caused some prosceniums and organ grilles to be destroyed. On the other hand, introducing four-channel magnetic sound printed on the film proved to be a major breakthrough for theatre sound. This system provided a left, center, and right channel plus one surround channel (Freeburg, "20th Century's Fortunes Tied to 3-D Movies").

Twentieth Century-Fox was convinced the success of CinemaScope "could turn the tide of pending economic disaster to the in-dustry as a result of television." The dramatic costume epic *The Robe*, the first Cinema-Scope feature film, was featured at the State-Lake Theatre on September 24, 1953.

Paramount Pictures responded by introducing VistaVision, a technique of optical reduction from a large negative image to the standard release print image. This process reduced grain, eliminated fuzziness, and gained a clearer picture. VistaVision was touted as the first process to make an improvement not only in picture quality, but in front and side seat viewing. *White Christmas* was the first film released in VistaVision in 1954.

Michael Todd, the Broadway producer, had been a partner in Cinerama Productions but wanted to find a way to achieve a similar effect more cheaply and easily. He wanted

State Street in 1957 looking south from Lake Street. Not only the Chicago and State-Lake, but the Loop, Oriental and Roosevelt theatres were featuring movies in color and CinemaScope.

to develop "a motion picture system that would photograph action in very wide angle with one camera on one strip of film to be projected from a single machine on a very large screen" (from the *Oklahoma!* brochure, 1955). His company enlisted the resources of the American Optical Company. The optical system developed centered around the famous 12.7-mm "Bugeye" lens that photographed an image 128 degrees wide, nearly "Cinerama outa one hole." The Todd-AO process used 70-mm film instead of the usual 35-mm and employed stereophonic sound using six separate sound tracks on the film ("Secret of New Movie System Is Wider Film," *Chicago Tribune*, 15 March 1956). The first Todd-AO film, *Oklahoma!* premiered at the McVickers in December 1955.

There seemed to be agreement among the studios and exhibitors that big screens, preferably seamless, and good projection equipment, lenses and adequate screen illumination were now essential for theatre owners. However, starting in the 1950s, due to the expense involved in achieving these standards, smaller theatres were forced to close, some never to reopen. Downtown movie theatres and playhouses would continue to lose audiences. The playhouses, too, began to disappear one by one; the building of single-screen theatres was over.

The "Loop Movie Schedule" in the late 1950s listed *Around the World in 80 Days* at the Cinestage and *South Pacific* at the McVickers, both in color and Todd-AO. Cinerama films were still at the Palace Theatre, which advertised "The Only Cinerama Theatre Within 300 Miles." The United

Artists advertised first-run films, and the Woods presented *Teacher's Pet* in VistaVision. The World Playhouse screened foreign films, while the Monroe advertised two science fiction-horror films. A rerelease of Walt Disney's *Snow White and the Seven Dwarfs* was at the Garrick. Film festivals continued at the Clark Theatre.

"Theater Drought of 1957 City's Longest of Century," wrote William Leonard in the *Chicago Tribune* (22 September 1957). The year 1932 had seen a six-week drought, but that was understandable because of the Great Depression. In 1918 no legitimate theatre in the Loop was open by order of the health department because of the influenza epidemic.

The Apollo and LaSalle theatres had closed in 1949. 1958 was the year the Harris closed as a playhouse; its twin, the Selwyn, had closed two years earlier. In April 1958, "Wrecking Crews Dropped the Final Curtain" on the Grand, Chicago's oldest continuous showplace. December 1958 found the Auditorium still closed. The Great Northern would close next in 1959. The historic Erlanger's final curtain was the night of March 10, 1962.

Three playhouses remained open during the 1950s and 1960s: the Studebaker, Shubert, and Blackstone theatres. Most musicals played at the Shubert while the Blackstone was established as the Chicago home of long-run comedies. The Studebaker featured both comedies and dramas. The Civic Theatre was too small for large stage productions. The McVickers presented the stage productions of *Fiddler on the Roof* and *Man of La Mancha* in the 1960s but then returned to featuring movies. The Auditorium reopened in 1967 with a performance by the New York City Ballet Company.

By the 1970s, the Loop had been bypassed for redevelopment in favor of North Michigan Avenue. Stores on North Michigan Avenue and in suburban shopping centers were luring customers away from State Street with film exhibitors following along. The downtown of the 1940s and 1950s had disap-

peared. The movie theatres that remained open into the 1970s often featured films with adult themes of sex and violence. Instead of staying downtown after work to have dinner and see a movie, people left. Some said they were afraid to stay downtown after dark.

In January 1975, one look at the "Amusements Downtown" listed in the *Chicago Tribune* told the story of what was happening in the Loop. Plitt Theatres now managed the Michael Todd, United Artists, Chicago, Roosevelt, and State-Lake theatres. During the third week of January 1975 the Monroe, State-Lake, McVicker's, Michael Todd, Cinestage, and Today theatres were closed for "fire code violations." The Monroe Theatre had been showing X-rated movies, as had the Rialto Theatre. The Cinestage called itself "Chicago's Leading Adult Theatre." The Essaness Woods Theatre was showing the latest Bond movie and eventually would feature martial-arts/action fare. The McVickers and Oriental were featuring kung fu films, as was the State-Lake Theatre.

After civic and business leaders complained that the Loop needed more glamour and amenities if it was to hold its own against North Michigan Avenue and suburban competition, a plan was conceived in 1974 to bring a new look to State Street. Completed in November 1979, the mile-long State Street Mall was considered the heart of downtown revitalization with a promenade of sidewalks, trees and greenery, benches, kiosks and escalators for the elevated tracks and shelters for bus riders. This was considered just one of the improvements planned for downtown. "Among the most important was said to be the building of a new Loop College at the south end of State Street and an urban renewal project at the north end of the Loop" (Gapp, "Merchants Optimistic"). The only motor vehicles allowed on the street were public buses and emergency vehicles. The goal was to bring life back to "that great street." But the jackhammers, dust, and torn-up pavement did nothing to contribute to people coming downtown.

In 1979, Chicago elected Jane Byrne its first woman mayor. At one of her early press conferences, Mayor Byrne heard complaints about the filthy conditions in Chicago's existing downtown theatres. This prompted the closure of the State-Lake, Oriental, and Roosevelt theatres by the city. Plitt Theatres terminated their lease of the Roosevelt Theatre, which closed September 1, 1979, amid reports that several movie houses were to be razed as part of a proposed North Loop Renewal Project. Since 1971, six other Loop theatres had either closed their doors or had been demolished: the Palace, Michael Todd, Monroe, Clark, Loop, and Today theatres. "Gone were the days when Chicago's downtown was the capital of Midwest movie going," wrote movie critic Gene Siskel in the *Chicago Tribune*.

In September 1985 plans were announced for a third restoration of the Chicago Theatre. Only three operating movie theatres remained in the Loop: the Cinestage, the United Artists, and the Woods theatres. The theatres had become dilapidated, their lobbies dominated by the candy counter and a row of video games. The Cinestage had screened adult films and closed a month later in October 1985. Kung fu and action films were on the screens of the Woods and United Artists theatres then owned and operated by Cineplex Odeon. The United Artists Theatre closed in 1988. In 1989, the Woods Theatre, on the northwest corner of Randolph and Dearborn streets, closed and soon thereafter was demolished. Chicago's Loop was without a movie theatre for the first time since the beginning of the century. A massive public effort had saved the Chicago Theatre, which became a performing arts venue.

When the Blackstone closed in 1988, the Shubert and the small Civic were the only playhouses downtown. The Civic Opera House, Orchestra Hall, and the Auditorium continued to present opera, concerts, and ballet, with the Auditorium now home to the Joffrey Ballet.

In 1989, the remainder of the block bounded by State, Dearborn, Washington, and Randolph Streets was razed as a result of redevelopment plans to revitalize the Loop's north end. This was an entire city block in the center of the Loop, part of the old Rialto. Referred to as Block 37, it took its name from the original fifty-eight city blocks established in 1830. In its prime, the block held a variety of establishments including movie theatres, retail stores, restaurants, the first skyscrapers of the 1890s, and what might be called the first gourmet food shop. The Roosevelt Theatre had been the first theatre to be demolished in the block, and when the block was leveled so was the United Artists Theatre.

Many delays halted any development plans for Block 37. For a decade it was used as an outdoor ice-skating rink in the winter and was the scene of various festivals and city events during warmer weather. (In 1996, State Street once again was open to traffic.) An office tower opened in 2008 with the new street-front studio and offices of WBBM-TV, Chicago's CBS affiliate (Manor, "Vision for the Loop"). Then in 2009, Block 37 opened: a glass-enclosed mall, five stories high, with high-end shops and restaurants having direct access to Chicago's Pedway (an underground walkway connecting Michigan Avenue to the Daley Center) and the subway system.

The development of a Randolph Street theatre district has once again revived State Street by bringing back to life not only its historic movie palaces, but by adding a new Goodman Theatre with the facades of the historic Harris and Selwyn theatres. These theatres complement the existing live entertainment venues in downtown Chicago: the Gene Siskel Film Center, the Bank of America and Auditorium theatres, Orchestra Hall, and the Civic Opera House. The two theatres in the Fine Arts Building at present are under restoration. The historic restored movie palaces, the Chicago, Oriental (Ford Center for Performing Arts), and Palace (Cadillac Palace) theatres, continue to attract audiences, bringing back memories of all that the old Rialto has seen during the last century.

Part II

THE THEATRES

The Theatres as They Opened After the Great Fire

New plans for the future were formed quickly after the Great Fire of 1871. James H. McVicker was the first to rebuild his destroyed theatre. Newly built theatres and music halls quickly followed to provide entertainment for Chicagoans, and toward the turn of the century dime museums and penny arcades became popular and dotted the downtown.

1857, 1872, 1891, 1922
McVickers Theatre

The first McVicker's Theatre, at 25 West Madison Street (between Dearborn and State streets) was built by James H. McVicker, a prominent Chicago actor. Designed by Otis L. Wheelock in an Italianate style, the theatre was opened on November 5, 1857, by a stock company with Mr. McVicker himself taking part in the opening presentation of *Honeymoon*, with an afterpiece called *The Rough Diamond*. It is recorded also that the entire company assembled on the stage and delighted the audience with the then new and popular melody "The Star-Spangled Banner." "For the first time since Chicago took rank as one of the first cities of the Union she has a theatre worthy of her citizens who patronize the drama" ("History of the Famous Theater," *Chicago Daily Tribune*, 27 August 1890). John Wilkes Booth appeared on stage in Shakespeare's *Richard III* in 1862. The touring company of the nation's first musical comedy, *The Black Crook*, appeared on stage for fifty-six performances. Mr. McVicker remodeled the theatre in 1864 and again in August of 1871. On October 9, 1871, the Great Chicago Fire completely destroyed the theatre.

The second McVicker's, another legiti-mate theatre, opened on August 20, 1872, with *Might Makes Right*. The theatre, designed by Wheelock & Thomas, was rebuilt in even grander style becoming one of the first new buildings to open after the Great Fire. The front entrance of the theatre was on Madison Street, but exits opened upon alleys on the east, west, and south sides. The lower floor contained the orchestra circle with 768 seats, while the first balcony contained 448 seats, and the second balcony 500. Its stage hosted Sarah Bernhardt's first Chicago appearance in 1881.

The theatre was reconstructed by Louis Sullivan in 1885, and it was said that his stylized stencil work echoed the designs used in the Auditorium. Theatregoers remarked on the light appearance of the interior. Additional exits were added so that all aisles led directly to doors. However, the second Mc-Vicker's burned down on August 26, 1890.

The third McVicker's reopened on Easter Sunday, 1891, with the Jefferson-Florence Company in *The Rivals*. There were a total of 1965 seats, including those in the two balconies and the gallery. A Roosevelt theatre organ was installed in the theatre, only the third organ in an American theatre. Five steel columns filled with concrete were placed on either side of the theatre to support the iron-trussed roof. The stage was enlarged, the box office was moved and two elevators were now part of the building. A new system of ventilation was installed as were leather-backed opera chairs ("Enter — New McVicker's," *Chicago Daily Tribune*, 22 March 1891).

The Iroquois Theatre fire prompted Mayor Harrison in 1904 to close every theatre until they complied with the new city ordinances. The McVickers installed new sprinklers and a steel curtain, after which proprietor Jacob Litt advertised new programs in "the safest theatre in the world" ("Every Theater in the City Shut by Mayor's Order," *Chicago Daily Tribune*, 3 January 1904).

In 1913, the theatre became part of the Jones, Linick and Schaefer circuit, and would join the ranks of the "10–20–30" vaudeville and moving picture theatres despite the fact that Mr. McVicker's will stated that the the-atre never be used for anything but high-class legitimate attractions.

The fourth McVickers Theatre was built in a classical style with a facade featuring a row of large Ionic columns, and mythological figures depicted on the pediment and friezes. A marquee stretched across the building on Madison Street, and an enormous vertical sign rose above the building's cornice. With an interior color scheme of mulberry and gold, the seating capacity was now 1,975. The older building was demolished so that Jones, Linick and Schaefer could rebuild a "movie palace" to showcase movies from Paramount Studios, having secured the exclusive rights for the Loop. The circuit then moved their corporate offices to the McVickers Building from the Rialto Theatre building.

The third McVickers Theatre was rebuilt by Adler and Sullivan on the same site as the first two McVicker's Theatres.

On February 1, 1926, the McVickers became a Balaban and Katz theatre. The seating capacity was now 2,264. On August 3, 1928, the gangster film *Lights of New York* premiered at the McVickers as the first all-talking (all-dialogue) feature. A new movie era was beginning (Tinee, "Crowds Stand in Line to Hear First Talkie"). Stage shows were presented with a full orchestra conducted first by Paul Ash before he moved to the Oriental Theatre.

"The combination of Shakespeare's plays and movies at the McVickers was a new event in the theater," said the director of the Old Globe Theatre productions. The critics called Mr. Jones' experiment "exciting." A preview was held on December 9, 1934 (*Chicago Tribune*), combining a new feature film on its screen with plays of Shakespeare in brief form as staged at "A Century of Progress." Aaron J. Jones had resumed control of the McVickers under a contract with its former operators, Balaban and Katz. (Collins, "Movie Theater

Will Offer Old Globe Players"). In 1937 the McVickers celebrated their eightieth anniversary. In 1947, even though Balaban and Katz owned 50 percent of the McVickers, it took no part in its management. That "released (the theatre) from the two feature (film) curb" ordered for Balaban and Katz theatres ("Loop Theater Released from Two Feature Curb," *Chicago Daily Tribune*, 21 November 1947).

In 1955 Aaron Jones Jr. announced that the McVickers would close on November 15 following the showing of *Queen Bee* to bring another innovation in motion pictures to Chicago ("McVickers Will Show Oklahoma Film on Dec. 26," *Chicago Tribune*, 6 November 1955).

The McVickers presented the first Chicago showing of Rodgers and Hammerstein's *Oklahoma!*, starting December 26, 1955, on a reserved-seat basis. The film introduced the new filmmaking process of Todd-AO, a high-definition wide-screen film format with a six-channel, high fidelity sound track. The Todd-AO system used to film *Oklahoma!* was developed by Michael Todd. He called it "Cinerama outa one hole." A new main floor projection booth was built for the Todd-AO equipment. *South Pacific* in Todd-AO was featured in 1958.

In 1959, the McVickers hosted a second showing of CineMiracle's *Windjammer* (first shown at the Civic Opera House the previous year). In December 1961 the lease was taken over from Jones, Linick & Schaefer by David and James Nederlander and Herman Bernstein. For a short time the theatre returned to presenting plays. January 30, 1962, marked the reopening of the McVickers refurbished as a legitimate theatre with *Do Re Mi* starring Phil Silvers and Nancy Kelley. In reviewing the performance, the *Chicago Tribune* reported (5 February 1962) that the

The fourth (to be last) McVickers opened October 26, 1922, designed by Thomas W. Lamb with Newhouse & Bernham associated.

"McVickers is small comfort for the city's loss of the Erlanger Theatre." Several more stage plays were presented but were not successful, leaving only the Shubert and Blackstone theatres in booking use for the 1962–1963 season (Cassidy, "On the Aisle").

During the summer of 1962 the McVickers was converted to the exclusive use of Cinerama. Because of technical improvements, only one projection booth was required. The McVickers had been leased for thirteen months by Martin Theatres of Columbus, Georgia, a large circuit with theatres primarily in the South ("Cinerama Will Reopen the McVickers," *Chicago Tribune*, 1 July 1962). The first three-strip Cinerama movie to tell a story, *The Wonderful World of the Brothers Grimm*, was presented on September 30, 1962. The McVickers was adver-

The proscenium of the (fourth) McVickers Theatre.

tised as the only theatre in Illinois able to show Cinerama movies. *Cheyenne Autumn*, photographed in Super Panavision 70 (a one-camera wide-screen process), was presented during November 1964 on a reserved-seat basis. On March 29, 1966, the McVickers hosted the world premier of three-strip Cinerama's *Russian Adventure* on a reserved-seat basis. (The movie was a compilation of Russian Kinopanorama films.) Cinerama productions at the McVickers ended the summer of 1966.

The McVickers presented two successful musicals: *Fiddler on the Roof* for thirty-seven weeks opening with the national touring company on February 1, 1967 (Leonard, *Chicago Tribune*, 29 January 1967) and the *Man of La Mancha* for an extended run still playing to crowds in 1968.

After that time the McVickers became part of Trans-Beacon Theatres, a circuit with theatres in Fresno and San Francisco, California; Columbus, Ohio; and Montreal, Canada. By 1970, the McVickers was screening rock westerns and X-rated films. The theatre closed on May 18, 1971, with manager Stuart Swanson citing declining revenues and excessive costs ("McVickers Theater to Close Tomorrow," *Chicago Tribune*, 17 May 1971). The McVickers reopened later in 1971 when a new labor contract had been signed.

In 1972 the stage production of *Purlie* received great reviews, which was followed by Theodore Bikel in *The Rothschilds* (Leonard, "There's Corn Amid the Cotton at McVickers"). During 1974, closed circuit telecasts were featured of the George Foreman-Norton and the Foreman-Muham-

The banner advertising the 1932 drama directed by Ernst Lubitsch for Paramount Pictures. The merger with Famous Players-Lasky gave Balaban & Katz access to Hollywood's top films.

mad Ali fights. The McVickers closed for good in 1984 and was demolished shortly thereafter. The building had been condemned citing an ornate interior in disrepair and a facade in danger of collapsing. This was the oldest theatre in Chicago, the third oldest in the nation.

1872 Myers' Opera House/
1874 Chicago Museum

Work continued by gaslight to ready the theatre before the first anniversary of the Great Fire. The "pretty little theatre" on Monroe Street near State Street opened September 23, 1872, with a minstrel troupe under the direction of Messrs. Arlington, Cotton, and Kamble. Before the Great Chicago Fire burned it down, Samuel Myers'

minstrel troupe performed at the popular Dearborn Theatre.

Myers' Opera House was directly in the rear of the McVicker's Theatre. The Monroe Street entrance was eighteen feet wide and about twenty feet in height. The auditorium was reached by a passage forty-five feet long at the end of which was a flight of steps that brought the patron to the level of the rear row of seats in the auditorium. At the foot of the steps was the ticket office on the left side of the vestibule. Stairs just outside the folding doors of the auditorium led to the gallery. The seating accommodated 1,100. The stage could be seen from every seat in the house, and two proscenium boxes were on each side of the stage. The frescoes were the work of Schubert and Koenig who also were responsible for the ornamentation in the McVicker's

The marquee's large panel advertised director John Ford's last Western.

strels. When it was swept away by the Great Fire of October 1871, Mr. Hooley built a new theatre at what is now 124 West Randolph Street. Hooley's opened with the Abbott-Kiralfy pantomime production of *The Black Crook* on October 21, 1872. Harry J. Powers was the theatre's manager. Handsome gasoliers provided light in the auditorium, first, and second balconies. The grand entrance to the four-story building was twenty feet wide by seventy feet in length. Another exit through an alley onto LaSalle Street was constructed later. A remodel of the theatre in August 1882 was the work of Dankmar Adler.

In 1898, the theatre was reconstructed and redecorated by Wilson and Marshall when Mr. Powers acquired the theatre and renamed it the Powers' Theatre. The prevailing colors were "Indian red, gold, ivory, and Osage green in the style of Louis IV" (*Chicago Tribune*, 31 March 1900). John Mears was manager. The orchestra was out of sight under the floor, and new large roomy seats were added, 1,250 in all. The most illustrious actors of the time preferred to appear at Powers' Theatre.

The Sherman House Hotel, reconstructed in 1911 by new owner Joseph Beifeld, was adjacent to the Powers' Theatre, which closed in 1924 to allow for the expansion of the hotel in 1925. The Sherman Hotel eventually took up the entire city block, but it closed in 1973 and was demolished in 1980. The site is now the home of the James R. Thompson Center, State of Illinois building, designed by Helmut Jahn.

Theatre. Samuel Myers died in June 1874; his Opera House closed November 28, 1874.

A month later, on December 14, 1874, it opened reconstructed into the Chicago Museum with a first-class collection of curiosities including a live alligator for one, and the comedy company of J. W. Blaisdell performing in the theatre. Mr. H. H. Peck was the proprietor with Mr. R. J. Waters the manager.

1872 Hooley's Theatre/
1898 Powers' Theatre

A year before the fire, Richard M. Hooley purchased Thomas Bryan's 1860 Concert Hall on Clark Street opposite the courthouse to build an opera house to present his min-

Top: Interior detail before demolition. *Bottom:* The interior in the early stages of demolition with a view of its decorative stair railings (McVickers Theatre).

1872 Aiken's Theatre/
1874 Adelphi Theatre

Frank E. Aiken also had his previous theatre destroyed by the Great Fire. On October 7, 1872, his new theatre on the northwest corner of Congress and Wabash Avenue opened designed by G. H. Edbrooke. Three towers rose up from the roof. A center tower rose nineteen feet over the cornice with the two corner towers rising twelve feet. The three-story building had three front entrances on Wabash Avenue and two exits on Congress Street. Two staircases each were available from the two upper balconies. The ticket office was in the middle of the vestibule. "Aiken's Theatre" was inscribed above the main entrance in capital letters ("Amusements," *Chicago Daily Tribune*, 9 October 1872).

The theatre closed February 2, 1873, after struggling with poor attendance, possibly due to bad weather, strong counter attractions, or being in an outlying location. Hereafter the theatre was rented for transient entertainment that desired an elegant auditorium, comfortable seats, and a large stage. A month later, Aiken's Theatre reopened.

Purchased by Mr. Leonard Grover, the theatre was renovated and rechristened the Adelphi Theatre opening February 2, 1874, with a variety program. The theatre may have remained open only until the end of May when it would have closed for the summer.

1864, 1875, 1884
Col. Wood's Museum

Opening on March 22, 1864, on the corner of Clark and Randolph, Col. John H. Wood's Museum was called the "showplace of the city." Curiosities, a panorama of London, and paintings of Indians were on display. Several halls were converted into a theatre with a seating capacity of 1,500. The building burned to the ground in the Great Chicago Fire, but a week later Col. Wood leased the Globe Theatre on Des Plaines Street, just outside the downtown area for a new museum (Wiedrich, "Enchantment of Wood's Museum Recalled").

The Chicago Museum had been open only a short time but standing vacant when Col. Wood rented the museum and reopened it on July 30, 1875, with "a good stock company and a fine assortment of curiosities charging twenty-five cents." The Wood's Museum took up the second to fourth floors. In the theatre on the second floor there was one gallery with 258 seats above the main floor, which had 432 seats. The upper floors held birds, rabbits, foxes, and two black bears. There was also a floor of stuffed specimens. The only entrance and exit from the auditorium was by means of a hall from Monroe Street, which contained the ticket office and a stairway. Tony Denier became manager in September 1877, but in the early morning of October 23, 1877, a fire broke out and the headlines in the *Chicago Tribune* read "Wood's Museum Is a Mass of Ruins." There were no plans to reopen the museum since it had been failing.

On January 3, 1884, Col. J. H. Wood secured the lease for museum and theatrical purposes of the Olympic Theatre Building on Clark Street. The portion of the theatre building that had been offices was turned into curiosity rooms. Four upper floors of the building were devoted entirely to museum purposes and contained many curiosities, mechanical novelties, and a collection of waxworks. A restaurant on the first floor remained.

Col. Wood's Museum opened April 12, 1884, making the location the largest amusement resort in the city (*Chicago Daily Tribune*, 12 April 1884). The entrance was on Randolph Street, a few doors east of Clark, and the exit at the one previously used by the Olympic Theatre. The entire building was "newly fitted up in an attractive style," with an additional gallery added to the theatre increasing the seating capacity to 1,000. The play *The Veteran* opened the theatre.

1873 Kingsbury Hall/1875 New Chicago Theatre/1878 Metropolitan/1879 Olympic Theatre/1928 Apollo Theatre

The first Kingsbury Hall had been dedicated on April 30, 1860, but burned down in the Great Fire of 1871 as did the other public halls. The Music Hall/Kingsbury Building was built in 1872, five stories high, on the northeast corner of Clark and Randolph streets. At the rear of the building, Kingsbury Hall opened on July 11, 1873, designed by Burling and Adler, with the entrance from 165 North Clark Street. The Theodore Thomas orchestra played their first performance at the Hall in October 1873. This was Chicago's first symphony orchestra. Three sides held the gallery with a dome of stained glass. The stage was fifty-six feet wide and twenty feet in depth. Galleries were reached by stairways at the north and south end of the hall. When Kingsbury Hall was built, only one building on Clark Street and one building on Randolph Street adjoined the hall. In May of 1874 *Little Red Riding Hood*, a pantomime with lifelike marionettes was presented and enthusiastically written about by Charles Dickens.

On August 16, 1875, James H. McVicker renamed the theatre the New Chicago, which was first known for its minstrel shows. The principal entrance to the auditorium was by means of a hallway eighty feet long from the Clark Street entrance. There was one gallery of 258 seats above the main floor of 432 seats, making a total of 984 seats. Mr. Walker became manager presenting German dramatic productions on Sunday. On September 16, 1878, Wurster's German theatre presented dramas and operettas. Music by Prof. Rosenbecker's Chicago Orchestra was performed between acts.

William Emmett of the Academy of Music renamed the theatre Metropolitan on November 10, 1878, and presented a variety show at its opening. Less than a year later,

under the management of Messrs. Mitchell and Sprague, the theatre was renamed the Olympic, opening with a "first-class" variety show and orchestra. The *Chicago Daily Tribune* critic wrote that "no such entertainment had been offered since Len Grover started the old Adelphi" (31 August 1879).

In 1896 a twelve-story, fireproof addition to the Ashland block at 74 West Randolph Street provided the Olympic with a large entrance twenty-five feet high fitted with mirrors, marble, and additional stairways. On April 3, 1904, the Olympic reopened with an innovative vaudeville program consisting of two performances in the afternoon and two performances in the evening. This was considered the first home of continuous vaudeville in Chicago (*Chicago Daily Tribune*, 29 January 1922). Managers Kohl and Castle would often close the 1,994-seat Olympic for the summer in the early 1900s while their Chicago Opera House remained open.

On June 15, 1907, headlines in the *Chicago Daily Tribune* read "Olympic Theatre Ruined By Fire." Crossed electric wires between the first and second galleries were suspected to be the cause of the fire. The roof collapsed causing the north end wall to "bulge out." Work on reconstruction of the theatre began less than a month later.

The reopening of the Olympic Theatre on November 8, 1908, was as an English music hall with J. J. Murdock as manager. A comedy drama was offered along with a number of variety acts.

Redone in predominantly rose colors, the Olympic was the only vaudeville theatre with a lounging parlor offering refreshments for the ladies. Smoking was permitted in all parts of the theatre ("A Rose Pink Music Hall," *Chicago Daily Tribune*, 11 November 1908).

The Vitagraph production of *The Battle Cry of Peace* with Norma Talmadge shown on October 17, 1915, was the film's first Chicago presentation. The first war film to show an actual battle would "make people think about the dangers of being unprepared" (Kelly, "Flickerings from Filmland," 18 October 1915). The film turned the Olympic Theatre into a home for pictures with orchestral accompaniment.

After the Olympic was shuttered on March 27, 1927, the theatre was remodeled and renamed the Apollo, operated by the Shuberts as a legitimate theatre specializing in musicals. The reopening on November 15, 1928, presented *Front Page*. During the first half of 1929, Mae West was on stage in *Diamond Lil*.

Chicago's oldest playhouse was leased by Balaban and Katz on May 1, 1934, and extensively remodeled, which included the installation of an air-conditioning plant as they had done in the Garrick Theatre next door

(Chase, "Apollo Leased for Motion Pictures"). The Apollo reopened on August 22, 1934, as a movie house with 1,383 seats.

The Apollo closed on May 11, 1949. One month later the interior of the old theatre was destroyed by fire. A new Loop Greyhound bus station opened on March 20, 1953, occupying property that included the historic Ashland block (containing the Apollo Theatre), the Union Building, and eleven other buildings.

1875 Coliseum/1878 Hamlin's Theatre/1880 Grand Opera House/ 1912 George M. Cohan's Grand Opera House/1926 Four Cohans/ 1942 RKO Grand Theatre

1913 Olympic Theatre playbill.

On August 29, 1880, the *Chicago Daily Tribune* announced there would be "Changes in the Building of Grand Opera House; Formerly known as Hamlin's Theatre." John A. Hamlin opened the Coliseum on August 7, 1875, on the site of Tom Foley's Billiard Hall at 119 North Clark Street between Randolph and Washington streets. It was considered a "variety dive of low repute." The theatre was renamed Hamlin's and reopened on September 11, 1878.

The theatre was completely remodeled and extensively reconstructed under the supervision of Dankmar Adler and renamed the Grand Opera House with Harry L. Hamlin as manager. The opening presentation on September 6, 1880, was *The Child of the State*. The building was six stories high, opposite the new courthouse. The grand staircase was the interior's main feature with the auditorium enlarged by seven feet on each side and the aisles widened as well. Another gallery was added. The lobby was reduced to provide space for a foyer

as in the Central Music Hall. The most noteworthy features were the proscenium boxes and "fashionable gas fixtures" ("Hamlin's New Theatre," *Chicago Daily Tribune*, 9 May 1880). Six stairways led to galleries and exits.

The *Chicago Daily Tribune* reported on June 20, 1897, "that the Veriscope pictures of the Corbett-Fitzsimmons contests continued to draw immense audiences at the Grand Opera House." In June 1902, the original production of *The Wizard of Oz* had its premier at the Grand Opera House. Fred Stone, who originated the role of the Scarecrow in the original stage version, perfected that role while playing at the Grand the summer of 1902. Children would watch fascinated at his dressing room window as he got into his costume (Fields, *Fred Stone*). Exactly a year later, Victor Herbert's *Babes in Toyland* premiered at the Grand.

Top: Converting the Apollo to a motion picture theatre meant that the last home of legitimate drama on Randolph Street, part of the old "Rialto," was gone. *Bottom:* 1938 *Snow White and the Seven Dwarfs.*

Top: 1937 *The Awful Truth. Bottom:* 1939 *Pygmalion.* All of these films shown at the Apollo were nominated for Best Picture including *Snow White* on the previous page.

Al Jolson, Fannie Brice, George M. Cohan, and Katharine Cornell were just some of the voices heard on stage at the Grand Opera House.

When Mr. Hamlin left the Opera House in 1912 after thirty-two years, George M. Cohan and his partner, Sam Harris, leased the theatre on March 3, 1912, which was then called George M. Cohan's Grand Opera House. Seating capacity was 1,400. In the early 1920s the Grand presented dramas on stage and occasionally featured photoplays.

Remodeled and reconstructed by architect Andrew N. Rebori, the theatre reopened, renamed the Four Cohans, on May 1, 1926, with the comedy *The Home-Towners*. By August, Messrs. Shubert and Cohan were jointly operating the theatre. When the Apollo was reconstructed into the United Artists Theatre, the Four Cohans, with its large stage, began to host the spacious shows once headed for the Apollo. On September 16, 1928, it was again called the Grand Opera

House and operated solely by the Shuberts (Hutchinson, "Finale Stirs Fond Memories of Old Grand").

The theatre was remodeled to show motion pictures and reopened in 1942 managed by RKO. Propelled by the box office boom of World War II and under new management, RKO Pictures made a strong comeback over the next half decade.

With the focus on star-driven features and some of the biggest names on loan from other studios, RKO pictures of the mid– and late forties offered Bing Crosby, Henry Fonda, John Wayne, and Ingrid Bergman among others. *The Bells of St. Mary's* in 1945 was the biggest hit of any in-house RKO production during the 1940s. RKO, and the movie industry as a whole, had its most profitable year ever in 1946. *The Best Years of Our Lives* was the most successful Hollywood

The Grand renamed the Four Cohans.

film of the decade. On Christmas Day 1946, *It's a Wonderful Life* had its Chicago premier at the Grand.

The theatre closed on March 31, 1958. RKO had stopped making pictures in 1957.

A week after the closing, headlines told the story: "Wrecking Crews Dropped the Final Curtain" (*Chicago Tribune*, 8 April 1958).

The City Hall Square Building stood next to the Grand Theatre and included the

The new, unusual RKO vertical sign reached the top of the building.

Palace Music Hall/Erlanger Theatre. In May of 1962 that entire block was demolished to make way for the Richard J. Daley Center (formerly the Chicago Civic Center).

1875 Adelphi Theatre/1877 Haverly's Theatre/1883 Columbia Theatre

After the Great Fire, J. H. Haverly's playhouse was built out of the walls left standing of the first custom house and post office built in 1857 for the village of Chicago. The northwest corner of Monroe and Dearborn had been the historical center from which the city grew from a struggling village. The "new" Adelphi Theatre opened January 11, 1875, at 57 West Monroe Street with an Italian opera and "Jack" Haverly's minstrels. It was the largest theatre erected until then with a seating capacity of 1,500 with only two exits. Besides a balcony and

The Grand awaiting its final curtain.

gallery, a still higher gallery, which held nearly 500 people, was suspended from the roof.

On August 5, 1877, Haverly's newly redecorated elegant theatre presented *Babes in the Wood* performed by Sam Colville's Folly Company. The exterior of the Lemont marble was cleaned as well as the French plate-glass windows on the facade. The walls were painted in a light mauve color with the fronts of the galleries and private boxes done in white and gold. The folding chairs were plush.

On January 25, 1879, with the opening of the operatic performances at Haverly's, the crowd was in excess of the safe capacity of the building. The theatre had been hurriedly

constructed, and even though the old post office walls were sound there was a good deal of apprehension as to the strength of the galleries, especially the one hung by iron rods from the roof without supports. Jack Haverly rebuilt the theatre in ninety days in 1880 for the start of the new fall season, which opened with a presentation of a *Comedy of Errors*. When Mr. Haverly went into debt, Will J. Davis was made manager.

Miss Ellen Terry, renowned stage actress, renamed the theatre in 1883 to the Columbia to signal the change of management. The six-story Columbia Theatre building was designed by Oscar Cobb, while the entrances were remodeled by Adler and Sullivan in 1884. A seating capacity of 2,400 included a balcony, gallery, and large auditorium. Every American player of prominence was seen on Columbia's stage, including Sarah Bernhardt in *Camille*, her last Chicago appearance in 1895. In later years the Columbia presented light musical attractions, and after closing for repairs for two weeks in August of 1890, it reopened with the comedy *The Country Fair*. In 1898, John Phillip Sousa's comic opera, *The Bride Elect*, was performed on stage.

The *Chicago Daily Tribune* of March 31, 1900, reported that a fire had started on the roof of the Monroe Street playhouse and the Columbia became "a heap of ruins within an hour."

The Inter Ocean Building, housing Chicago's daily morning newspaper, the *Inter Ocean*, was built on the site. The building would later be gutted and converted into the Monroe Theatre.

1879 Central Music Hall

Plans were started early in 1879 led by George B. Carpenter for the most perfect

The main entrance was on State Street with a frontage of 120 feet and depth of 150 feet. Steps from the sidewalk led up to the first floor. (Courtesy John Watson.)

music hall auditorium in the country. The upper floors of the six-story building would have seventy offices, music rooms and studios with fine stores on the ground-floor Randolph Street front. A marble corridor would lead back to the hall. In addition to a large lobby and foyer, a carriage arcade was included in the design so that carriages could drive into it from Washington Street and drive out on Randolph Street ("New Music Hall," *Chicago Daily Tribune*, 10 August 1879). Dankmar Adler designed the building with a combination of traditional masonry-bearing walls and internal iron members. The Central Music Hall was the forerunner of the Auditorium.

On December 8, 1879, Carlotta Patti formally dedicated the Central Music Hall to the musical public. Her concerts were a long-established favorite, and the hall was filled to capacity. In October 1880, a three-manual organ was installed. A smaller hall on the third floor of the State Street front seating 600 was adapted for chamber concerts.

In 1897, Burton Holmes' weekly lectures attracted large audiences that would fill the hall. His travel lectures were always accompanied by richly colored stereopticon views. "Among the moving pictures the football scrimmages on the University of Chicago campus in the Thanksgiving game aroused the greatest interest" (Burton Holmes' Third Talk," *Chicago Daily Tribune*, 27 November 1897).

Long a landmark in Chicago, the Central Music Hall closed with a benefit concert on April 28, 1901. Chicago had no hall to fill its place, for the Auditorium was too large and other halls too small ("The End of Central Music Hall," *Chicago Daily Tribune*, 28 April 1901). Central Music Hall, the National Life block, and Tribune offices were all razed to make way for the expansion of Marshall Field and Company, Chicago's largest de-

All 3,000 seats commanded an unrestricted view of the stage in the Central Music Hall.

partment store, on State Street. A massive, twelve-story building fronting on State Street was built in 1902, including a grand new entrance for Chicago's most famous department store.

1884 Casino Garden/1905 Brooke's Casino/1908 Garden Theatre/ 1909 American Music Hall/1915 Chicago Theatre/1918 Aryan Grotto Theatre /1924 Eighth Street Theatre

The panorama of the Battle of Gettysburg on display in the circular theatre on Wabash Avenue was generating so much excitement that businessmen, thinking that the neighborhood would become an amusement center, proposed that a casino building be built on the northeast corner of Wabash Av-

enue and Peck Court. On September 23, 1884, the plans drawn up included a theatre with an orchestra to present concerts on Sundays, and comic opera presentations at other times. Designed by architects Richard E. Schmidt, Garden and Martin, the building was three stories high with a summer roof garden.

A fine restaurant and first-class club rooms were connected to the theatre ("Casino Building," *Chicago Daily Tribune*, 23 September 1884). Brooke's Band became the feature attraction at the Casino Garden. By 1905 the theatre was renamed Brooke's Casino with the "Britt-Nelson Moving Fight Pictures" taken at ringside featured at the theatre in October of that year. Mr. Brooke also presented boxing and wrestling matches and a pool tournament. Brooke's Casino hosted the 1907 Democratic City Convention.

A new theatre, called the Garden, was rebuilt on the site because "Chicago was long known as the Garden City of the West." The interior was suggestive of a garden with terraces and promenades. The musical comedy *A Winning Miss* opened the newly renamed theatre on November 21, 1908, under the direction of Thomas J. Noonan, formerly business manager of the Illinois Theatre ("News of the Theaters," *Chicago Daily Tribune*, 22 November 1908). A double tier of boxes, like the Auditorium Theatre, extended from the band shell to its rear wall. The new music hall was influenced by Parisian designs. The "indoor/outdoor" theatre had two large papier-mâché trees on either side of the proscenium arch. A row of trees lined the sides of the auditorium so that the branches would "intermingle" on the ceiling. "Through this canopy incandescent stars in purplish tint twinkled with a harvest moon at the right corner" (Hubbard, "News of the Theaters").

Top: On April 16, 1924, the classic *The Hoosier Schoolmaster* was the feature to open the newly renamed Eighth Street Theatre. *Bottom:* According to WLS, nearly three million people attended the Barn Dance performances at the Eighth Street Theatre during its twenty-five-year run.

The Garden passed from the hands of the Elysian Garden Company and manager Thomas J. Noonan into the hands of William Morris, independent vaudeville magnate. Monday evening, January 18, 1909, marked the beginning of Chicago's newest vaudeville theatre, the American Music Hall. The theatre was reconstructed to include a balcony. Ten vaudeville acts were presented with prices ranging from fifty cents to $1.50. At the very end of the program was "Morriscope," a series of moving picture comedy shorts. Tea and cakes were presented to ladies

The Eighth Street Theatre sported a new facade during the 1940s.

during matinee intermissions (*Chicago Daily Tribune*, 20 January 1909). In January 1911, the hall passed into the possession of the American Music Hall Company with George A. Harrison as the new manager.

Renamed the Chicago Theatre, the opening program on Christmas Eve 1915 was the play *Within the Loop*. A musical comedy *Katinka* played in January 1917 featuring the cast from the Garrick Theatre. A *Chicago Tribune* article of July 23, 1917, reported that the owners of the Chicago Theatre said they would make an effort to keep the house going; Messrs. Shubert's lease had expired some months back.

The Aryan Grotto Temple Association purchased the Chicago Theatre building on June 18, 1918, with the intention of using the building for lodge meetings and conventions. The Aryan Grotto was an organization of Masons, famous in the Midwest for its picturesque pageants. In 1922 and 1923, the

Aryan Grotto Theatre presented both stage plays and films ("Theater Notes," *Chicago Daily Tribune*, 14 December 1922).

Chicago radio station WLS (sponsored by the Sears Roebuck Agricultural Foundation) aired the first National Barn Dance program on April 19, 1924. The four hours of fiddle music, comedy and down-home entertainment were aimed at rural audiences. Studios were on the second floor of the Sherman House Hotel. The program went on to become one of the most popular and longest running country-and-western shows in history. By March 1932, the National Barn Dance program was cut to two hours and broadcast live from the Eighth Street Theatre. Thousands came to fill the 1,200-seat theatre every Saturday night.

During World War II, the theatre was used as an Army Technical Training Center as were the adjacent Stevens Hotel (now Chicago Hilton), Chicago Coliseum, and the Congress Hotel. In 1944, Paramount Pictures made a film called *National Barn Dance* that fictionalized the creation of the show and featured many of its stars.

The Joffrey Ballet's first performance in a major city was at the Eighth Street Theatre on January 22, 1957. Faced with dwindling audiences, WLS closed down the live broadcasts of the National Barn Dance on August 31, 1957. The theatre was razed in 1960 for an addition to the convention facilities of the Hilton Hotel.

1885 Chicago Opera House

The Chicago Opera House opened on August 18, 1885, on the site of the old Tivoli

Building with Thomas Keene in *Hamlet*. The theatre's 1,600 seats were filled. The building at 111 Washington Street was ten stories, 140 feet high on spread foundations. This was the first fireproof theatre in Chicago designed by Cobb and Frost. For ten years, managed by David Henderson, the Chicago Opera House was known as the greatest producing house of extravaganzas in the United States. Madame Modjeska was seen on its stage, as was the first presentation of the Wagnerian cycle, *Der Ring des Nibelungen*. In 1890 patrons saw a Gilbert and Sullivan light opera. The theatre in 1895 was under the management of Messrs. Kohl and Castle. Vaudeville acts and comedy productions were presented until July 30, 1908, when Klaw and Erlanger became associated with the management of the Chicago Opera House. The Washington Street playhouse was renovated and redecorated, presenting dramas with a sprinkling of musical comedy.

When the Chicago Opera House closed in 1912, it was demolished to make way for what would be Daniel Burnham's last building: the Conway Building, completed in 1913. The building was developed by the Marshall Field Estate and named for his birthplace, Conway, Massachusetts. Designated a historic landmark in 1984, the site is now called Burnham Center. All four corners of the building are rounded. Originally the light court in the center of the building penetrated down to a skylight over the lobby, but the third through the seventh floors were later extended over the opening.

1888 Eden Musee/1894 Casino Theatre

On January 1, 1888, the property at 227–229 Wabash Avenue near Jackson Street was leased to the Chicago Panoptican Company. They erected a four-story building and opened Eden Musee, which became a popular dime museum. Two thousand guests were invited to the opening of the Eden Musee on June 16, 1888, to view the representations of historical scenes and persons on display. The

basement held a "Chamber of Horrors." The museum closed its doors on July 1, 1894.

A remodeled theatre called the Casino opened on August 12, 1894. The theatre opened for the new fall season with a variety show accompanied by an orchestra. Frank Hall was the manager of this only all-day vaudeville theatre in Chicago. The main floor had been inclined and raised affording a better view of the now-enlarged stage.

On March 14, 1897, the Empire Theatre Company bought the Casino property and leased it to the Hartman Company for expansion of their retail clothing store.

1889 Auditorium Theatre

Dankmar Adler and Louis Sullivan's masterpiece, the Auditorium Theatre, is at 50 East Congress Parkway, on the corner of Michigan Avenue. The theatre was designed to be the centerpiece of a hotel and office tower building, a complex multiuse building. The two architects were at the height of their creative powers.

Before the official opening, the Auditorium, with a makeshift roof, was host to the 1888 Republican National Convention with Benjamin Harrison emerging as the party's candidate. Victorious, President Harrison returned a year later to dedicate the Auditorium to an overflowing crowd with more than a thousand people sitting on stage (Naylor and Dillon, *American Theaters Performance Halls of the Nineteenth Century*). Risers could be added to the lobby of the dress circle, stage, or hallways behind the boxes to increase the seating capacity to 6,000.

President Harrison dedicated the new building on December 9, 1889. The next day the Auditorium was opened as a home of opera with Gounod's *Romeo and Juliet*. The scenery for the Italian opera was painted in Vienna.

At the time, it was the tallest building in Chicago and the most massive piece of architecture in the modern world with a 400-room hotel and 136 offices and retail stores.

Often called "America's Most Beautiful Theatre," the largely granite and limestone Romanesque theatre building fills an entire block in Chicago's Loop.

The hotel fronted on Michigan Avenue (now Roosevelt University). The tall eighteen-story tower block is on the west side of the building, with the rest of the building ten stories high (Roth, *A Concise History of American Architecture*).

The Auditorium has been called the world's most acoustically perfect building. Dankmar Adler was responsible for the acoustics as well as the theatre's innovative hydraulic lifts to move scenery, the first central air-cooling system, an inner proscenium frame used to reduce the stage opening, and drop-down ceiling panels to close off the fronts of the two top galleries for more intimate performances. On the first balcony, curtains could be lowered between pillars to close off the back half of the seats, thus decreasing the seating of the theatre to 2,500 for smaller events. Dankmar Adler wanted the Auditorium to be a "people's theatre" with many inexpensive seats. Frank Lloyd Wright was quoted as saying, "the greatest

room for music and opera in the world — bar none" (Henning, "Form Follows Function, Elegantly").

Louis Sullivan's dictum that "form follows function" is on display in the interior of the Auditorium, considered one of his masterpieces. A low, arched proscenium and a ceiling that gradually heightens as it recedes in several arches is a design unprecedented in the late nineteenth century. This was the first theatre shaped like a cone. The main floor and balcony with 4,237 seats are set in sweeping curves.

The boxes are set off by cast-iron arches and railings that echo the patterns in the ceiling. Sullivan's floral decorations were inspired by Byzantine motifs. Mosaic marble floors can be seen throughout the theatre, its lobbies and foyers. Over the doors, at the building's entrance, are six arched art glass lunettes inspired by the allegorical figures of Wisdom, Oratory, Drama, Music, Poetry and Dance.

The theatre became the home of the

Chicago Symphony Orchestra, the Chicago Opera Company, and Mary Garden's Opera Company. However, in 1904 manager Wessels reported that the Chicago Symphony would be leaving and taking up its new home in the newly opened Orchestra Hall.

The movie *The Unbeliever*, produced by Thomas A. Edison Inc. in conjunction with the U.S. Marine Corps, was presented in April 1918.

Messrs. Shubert took over management of the Auditorium on September 1, 1924. On January

Top: The Auditorium was the first theatre entirely lit by (custom-manufactured) incandescent bulbs, with 3,500 along the ceiling arches and fronts of the balcony and galleries. *Bottom:* Music lovers considered the "peanut gallery" seats the best in the house.

AUDITORIUM THEATRE

Florenz Ziegfeld's musical play, *Show Boat*, was revived at the Auditorium in April 1933 shortly before his death. The music was by Jerome Kern.

26, 1929, the Chicago Civic Opera Company gave its last performance in the historic theatre (Moore, "Romeo and Juliet to Close Opera in Auditorium"). The new Civic Opera House had opened and would be ready for the fall season leaving the Auditorium without a regular tenant.

After several years of remaining closed, the Auditorium was redecorated by John Holabird and John Root. The marble stairs to the boxes and promenade were restored, and new velvet chairs were added. A concert on December 14, 1932, reopened the theatre. There followed attractions showcasing music and theatre productions with George A. Kingsbury as manager. Paderewski, with an

all-Chopin recital, was on stage during this period ("Good Omens in New Career of Old Auditorium," *Chicago Daily Tribune*, 2 April 1933). *Show Boat* was considered Mr. Ziegfeld's masterwork. The presentation allowed Chicagoans an opportunity to see a show produced and directed by Mr. Ziegfeld.

Ultimately, the Auditorium closed on June 30, 1941, being not profitable and with an accumulation of unpaid taxes. Fortunately, the Auditorium building, with its fortresslike architecture, would have been demolished, but costs were determined to be more than the land. During World War II, the Auditorium became a USO Center with the stage and main floor becoming a bowling alley. Parts of the building were used as barracks. In 1946, year-old Roosevelt College purchased the theatre and hotel, pledging to return the theatre to the world of music and cultural events ("Auditorium Is Bought by College," *Chicago Daily Tribune*, 6 August 1946).

The Auditorium was left empty and fell into disuse until the Auditorium Theatre Council was formed in 1960 to begin plans for renovation. Harry Weese was the architect heading the restoration effort to bring it back to its original form. The stage floor was replaced. When a row of boxes was removed that had been installed between the orchestra seats and the grand foyer, examples of Sullivan's stenciling and remnants of original paint were found. New chairs in the original design were installed.

On October 31, 1967, the Auditorium reopened with a performance by the New York City Ballet of *A Midsummer Night's Dream*. "Why don't they build like this today?" said its director, George Balanchine. "Nothing could be more modern than this."

The history of the Auditorium was said to be a catalogue of the American stage. Today, the theatre presents classical music, ballet, Broadway musicals, and is the permanent home of the Joffrey Ballet. Today, the Auditorium can seat 3,877 patrons during a single performance. Broadway in Chicago and the Auditorium Theatre of Roosevelt University joined together to form an unprecedented partnership between not-for-profit and for-profit. The two organizations have formed a long-term alliance that allows Broadway in Chicago the theatrical rights to book the Auditorium.

The Auditorium Theatre of Roosevelt University was listed on the National Register of Historic Places in 1970 and became a Chicago Landmark in 1976. It is an independent not-for-profit organization committed to presenting the finest in international, cultural and community programming in Chicago, and to the continued restoration and preservation of the only survivor of Adler and Sullivan's major works in Chicago.

1890 Crystal Palace Theatre/1903 Cleveland's Theatre/1906 International Theatre/1909 Globe Theatre/1915 Strand Theatre

Built by Bauer and Hill, the building on the southwest corner of Wabash and Hubbard Court was almost circular, a sixteen-sided polygon with a 135-foot diameter. The building had a wrought-iron frame and a dome roof that topped a cupola. The foyer was initially at the corner and tiled, which led to a narrow passageway to the center of the building. There a spiral staircase led to a forty-foot circular platform from which patrons could view the enormous 42 feet high by 365 feet in circumference cyclorama oil-on-canvas painting. The 360-degree cylindrical painting by artist Paul Philippoteaux of the *Battle of Gettysburg* depicted the final Confederate assault on July 3, 1863. The work took over a year and a half to complete (www.nps.gov/gett/historyculture-/gettysburg-cyclorama.htm).

The first public showing was on October 22, 1883, with the addition of a three-dimensional foreground littered with models and replicas of the relics of battle, stone walls, shattered trees, and broken fences to enhance the illusion of being in the center of a great historic scene. Visitors were awed by the painting's spectacular realism. This was the first of four versions and is one of only two surviving cycloramas in this country. The Chicago cyclorama was lost for some time but was rediscovered in 1965 and purchased by North Carolina investors in 2007. A second cyclorama is on display at the Gettysburg National Park Museum (www.gettysburg.edu/special_collections/contact.dot).

On April 30, 1890, the building was remodeled into a theatre called the Crystal Palace with a seating capacity of 1,250. Two balconies were above the main floor of the theatre; the first balcony was said to have the best seats in the house. The stage was forty feet in depth and width.

The W. S. Cleveland Amusement Company had Oscar Cobb redesign the theatre, and Cleveland's Theatre opened October 31, 1903, with the play *Magda*, featuring John Barrymore. Called Cleveland's in the playbill listing, the theatre now had 975 seats. The acoustics in the round building came to be a problem.

With improvements and renamed the International, the theatre reopened on May 13, 1906. Manager Cleveland promised "original greater vaudeville," including Thompson's elephants, and new moving pictures using the Optiscope. In 1907, *Rigoletto* opened an extended stay of the Italian Grand Opera Company. The next year on September 1, after a thorough renovation, the playhouse reopened presenting Yiddish drama by manager Ellis F. Glickman. When that was less than successful, English and Italian operas were presented at popular prices. However, on January 7, 1909, Manager Glickman announced there would be no more performances due to lack of support, and in April of that year due to persistent fire code violations, the mayor ordered the International to close.

An extensive structural and decorative remodeling reopened the theatre again in August 1909, now called the Globe Theatre. Managers Stair and Havlin promised come-

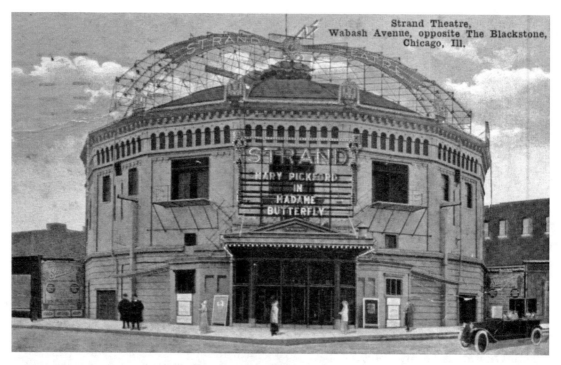

Top: On October 16, 1915, Geraldine Farrar appeared in the Paramount photoplay of *Carmen*, the opening feature of the newly renamed Strand Theatre. *Bottom:* On June 26, 1921, the *Chicago Daily Tribune* reported that "one of the most picturesque of the old amusement places was to be wrecked." (Postcards courtesy www.chicagopc.info.)

people to this somewhat out-of-the-way location. Opposite the Blackstone Hotel, the Strand advertised "Entire Bill Changed Every Monday." Saturday mornings were devoted to the "Children's Hour" for ten cents admission ("Farrar's *Carmen* Opens New Strand," *Chicago Daily Tribune*, 16 October 1915). "[It was] the Strand when it housed films, the theatre had presented vaudeville to grand opera with long intermissions of closed doors." A twenty-one-story office building was planned for the site ("Huge Building May Supplant Strand Theater," *Chicago Daily Tribune*, 26 June 1921).

dies, dramas, and musical plays. Wrestling matches were presented in 1913 and dramas in 1914.

A capacity house filled the walls of the extensively redecorated Strand Theatre on opening night. The feature film was presented with a Pathe scenic travel series, a comedy, and "topics of the day." Manager E. Cordner said such a program would bring

1892 Schiller Theatre/1898 Dearborn Theatre/1903 Garrick Theatre

Chicago's large German community wanted a permanent home for German drama in the Loop. Dankmar Adler and Louis Sullivan were commissioned, and "Chicago's handsomest playhouse" was built

("It Is Completely Fireproof," *Chicago Daily Tribune*, 30 September 1892). The Schiller building, at 64 West Randolph Street, with a frontage of eighty feet on Randolph, was a seventeen-story, completely fireproof steel frame building with the exterior faced with a light brown terra cotta and a darker reddish brown in the decorative trim. The front of the building was decorated with statues of twelve famous composers and musicians. A decorated cornice capped the tower. The Schiller was the last Adler and Sullivan theatre to be built, considered by some to be one of the masterpieces of the Chicago school of architecture. Marble and mahogany were used throughout the interior. All halls and corridors had mosaic floors. Concealed lights illuminated the ceiling. A seating capacity of 1,286 included three proscenium boxes on either side of the stage, a balcony and gallery. Columns were not needed to support the balconies because of the cantilever system used by Dankmar Adler.

The opening program on September 29, 1892, consisted of Weber's *Jubilation Overture*, poetry, songs, and the German drama *Gerade wie in Deutschland* (Just Like in Germany) performed in German. On October 2, 1892, Herr Wachsner opened a season of German drama beginning with the play, written in rhymes, *The Pioneers*. Two weeks later the Schiller presented its first show in English, a Charles Frohman farce, *Gloriana*. By the summer of 1893, with Sigmund Selig managing the theatre, the Schiller presented English-language plays during the week and German programs on the weekend. By 1895 the building was sold for not turning a profit, and a year later Cinematographe and vaudeville were advertised at the theatre. In 1898 the Schiller became the Dearborn Theatre.

The *Chicago Daily Tribune* reported that on September 5, 1898, to celebrate its new name, the Dearborn Theatre opened with the comedy drama *Too Much Johnson*, four

A series of eight arches radiating from the proscenium provided for excellent acoustics. This Richard Nickel view of Sullivan's ornamental work was taken during the television studio period.

vaudeville features, and new Biograph moving pictures of war scenes in Cuba. Tri-State Amusement Company now managed the theatre and planned to run the theatre at moderate prices. In 1899, the Dearborn dropped vaudeville from their entertainments and presented only dramas. Because the theatre couldn't compete with Kohl and Castle in securing good vaudeville talent, the last performance as the Dearborn Theatre was a benefit on August 30, 1903.

The Shubert Brothers acquired the theatre on September 1, 1903, renaming it after actor David Garrick. After the Iroquois fire in 1903, the mayor ordered every theatre in the city shut until they complied with new ordnances ("Every Theatre in the City Shut by Mayor's Order," *Chicago Daily Tribune*, 3 January 1904). The Garrick reopened with the play *Winsome Winnie* on February 1,

1904, to become a prominent theatre on the Rialto presenting the country's top stage productions with such stars as Lionel Barrymore, Mary Pickford, and Al Jolson. It was the flagship Shubert house in Chicago.

The future of the Garrick was foretold

A 1913 playbill from the Garrick Theatre.

when it presented two major motion pictures in the mid–1920s. *The Big Parade* in 1925 was considered one of the greatest hits of the 1920s because the film did not glorify the war. On November 29, 1927, on a reserved-seat basis, the Garrick held the gala premier of *The Jazz Singer* starring Al Jolson. The film was so successful that it played at the Garrick Theatre into 1928. The *Tribune*'s movie critic wrote that "the Vitaphone is cunningly utilized in some of the scenes and you HEAR the star sing some of his best-loved songs" (Tinee, "Jolson Magic Is Magic Still, Even in Movie").

The Shubert Theater Corporation was placed in equity receivership in 1931. New

owners later that year presented the play *Girl Crazy*, which ran for more than ten weeks. In December 1933, the curtain fell on *The Bartered Bride*, the last legitimate stage production at the theatre.

The Publix-Balaban and Katz Corporation leased the theatre on March 1, 1934, and had it remodeled as a movie theatre. The Garrick reopened on June 1, 1934, with the film *Wonder Bar* with Al Jolson. A. M. Strauss was responsible for the remodel that used aluminum and black Vitrolite to "modernize" what was felt to be an antiquated front. Columns were covered in steel and brass. Not only did this clash with Adler and Sullivan's original design, but erecting a new, larger marquee hid Sullivan's terra cotta decoration. Opera boxes were removed so more seats could be added. A projection booth was installed in the first balcony.

The pictures tell the story of Balaban and Katz's use of advertising banners becoming more extreme, with the columns wrapped just short of covering the entire facade. The featured films were also in direct contrast to their neighboring Apollo Theatre.

The Balaban and Katz Corporation had purchased the Garrick Theatre building on February 18, 1950. *Back to Bataan* and *Marine Raiders*, shown on August 10, 1950, were the last movies shown until 1957. During those years, the Garrick was converted into a television studio for WBKB and later for WBBM, Chicago's CBS affiliate. The first program televised from its stage on January 10, 1952, was entitled "The Pace of Chicago." A new stage had been built over the old orchestra section in an eighteen-foot semicircle, with three camera runways fanning out to leave room for only five rows of seats totaling 300 at the end of the platforms.

The Garrick became a movie house again on April 18, 1957, with the Midwest premier of *Fear Strikes Out*, based on the life of Jim Piersall, outfielder for the Boston Red Sox. However, the theatre was soon showing double features headed by *The Blood of the Vampires*. Even before the Garrick Theatre

Top: The remodeled "modern" entrance and marquee in 1934. *Bottom:* The 1936 musical comedy *Sing Baby Sing.*

Top: A drug addiction drama, the 1936 *Marihuana, was* meant to be an anti-weed documentary. *Bottom: Forbidden Adventure* (1937) was a legendary phony documentary. The film played on the exploitation circuit for years advertising its nudity (Garrick Theatre).

BooLoo — White Tiger God of the Sakai (1938) was filmed in the jungles of Malaysia.

officially closed in May 1960, Balaban and Katz claimed the "masterpiece" was "falling to pieces costing them $500 a day to maintain even when empty" ("Pride Is Held Last Hope of the Garrick," *Chicago Tribune*, 7 July 1960). They wanted to tear down the building and lease the land for a parking garage.

Richard Nickel, historian and photographer, organized one of the country's first protests in support of historic preservation. During the summer of 1960, attempts to save the historic Garrick Theatre building heated up (Indreika, "The History of the Schiller (Garrick) Theatre").

The *Chicago Tribune* reported on several attempts to save the Adler and Sullivan building. On May 26, 1960, Alderman Leon M. Despres asked Mayor Daley to take immediate steps to save the Garrick building.

The City Building Commission ruled on July 7 that it was economically unfeasible to recondition the building. Just over a week later a court order was requested to raze the Garrick. Judge Donald S. McKinley of the Superior Court prevented the razing, citing the "Save the Garrick" proponents who had been pleading for preservation of the building. By August 25, 1960, the City Council concluded that the building should be razed without delay. They argued that water seepage had corroded much of the building's steel supporting structure and had damaged the terra cotta masonry on the facade. The *Chicago Tribune* reported on November 23, 1960, that the court had reversed Judge McKinley's ruling. The Garrick building was demolished between January and June 1961. "An irreplaceable loss to the city's culture," Judge McKinley said.

Richard Nickel's view of the auditorium taken during the early 1950s.

Photographer Richard Nickel did rescue a portion of Sullivan's stencil work and floor landings containing rich mosaic designs ("Discover Long Hidden Art in Garrick Relics," *Chicago Tribune*, 26 July 1961). The front entrance of The Second City, the premier comedy theatre and school of improvisation in Chicago, contains the Louis Sullivan arches from the Garrick Theatre. The Art Institute of Chicago has fragments of the interior plasterwork and terra cotta. Additional pieces of ornamental artwork salvaged from the Garrick were sent to museums and educational institutions throughout the country including Yale and Harvard universities.

1896 Great Northern Theatre

The Great Northern Hotel expanded in 1885 by building an office building on the east side of the property, which included a theatre with an entrance at 21 West Quincy Street through a spacious lobby from Jackson Street. Mr. A. M. Palmer wanted a theatre built for his stock company and had John Burnham and John Root design the building.

The lobby led to a wide promenade extending nearly the entire length of the new building. Both lobby and foyer were paved with mosaics, and the walls and ceilings were of marble. The interior design included a large stage eighty-five feet wide with a cream and gold color scheme in the auditorium. The 1,400 seats were upholstered in crimson. The balcony was reached by two broad stairways, one to the east of each entrance.

The Great Northern Theatre opened November 9, 1896, with the premier production of *Heartsease* with Henry Miller. In 1897, David Henderson became manager of the theatre. The next year saw Salisbury and Tate turn the Great Northern into a vaudeville theatre. During the first years of the new century Messrs. Stair and Havlin operated the theatre, playing attractions a cut below the McVicker's. The presentations fluctuated between legitimate, vaudeville, movies, and stock company productions.

It was for a time operated by the Shuberts as the Lyric Theatre from February 1910, presenting comedy and character drama. The theatre had been redecorated with a new color scheme of gray and mulberry. The ushers served water and sold bonbons. The theatre was renamed the Hippodrome on November 11, 1912, when the theatre joined the two-a-day ranks. Gradually it was called the Great Northern Hippodrome for several years before becoming simply the Great Northern Theatre once more in September 1921, when Florence Reed opened in *The Mirage*. February 22, 1925, marked the Great Northern's broadcast from the theatre of Gilbert and Sullivan's *The Mikado* for WGN radio. Sigmund Romberg's musical romance, *The Student Prince*, also opened that month and ran fifty-nine consecutive weeks making theatrical history in Chicago ("Eight Years of Popularity for Student Prince," *Chicago Daily Tribune*, 12 February 1933). Vaudeville was never presented again.

The Blackstone and Great Northern theatres were two theatres that closed at the height of the Depression. In March 1936, these two theatres were reopened by a WPA program. The Great Northern was referred to as Federal Theatre No. 1 and presented Ibsen's *An Enemy of the People*. The drama had been performed at the theatre by the Moscow Art Theatre in 1923. The theatre underwent a facelift for the April 19, 1948, opening of *My Romance*. The Great Northern closed on November 22, 1959, with a performance by the Bayanihan dancers. The theatre was demolished in 1961 to make way for the new Dirksen Federal Building.

1895 Steinway Hall/1906 New Theatre/1907 Whitney's Opera House/1913 Howard's Comedy Theatre/1914 Comedy Theatre/1915

Central Music Hall/ 1920 Central Theatre/1930 Punch & Judy/ 1935 Sonotone Theatre/1940 Studio Theatre/ 1952 Ziegfeld Theatre/ 1958 Capri Theatre

The Chicago Musical College was built on this site in 1886 with Dr. Florenz Ziegfeld Sr. as its director. Steinway Hall, at the ground level of this eleven-story building at 64 East Van Buren Street near Michigan Avenue, would become the most renamed theatre in Loop history. The *Chicago Tribune* called it "the Chameleon Theatre" in 1941. The entrance was three stories high including a grand staircase to the recital hall. The style of architecture was said to be Italian Renaissance ("Building for the Music Folk," *Chicago Daily Tribune*, 2 September 1894). All 700 seats were filled in Steinway Hall on May 10, 1895, for the inaugural concert of the Chicago Orchestra under the direction of Theodore Thomas. The hall primarily hosted concerts, recitals, and lectures.

In May of 1906, the hall was enlarged and reconstructed under the direction of architects Marshall and Fox. Opening on October 8, 1906, as the New Theatre, the playhouse presented three short plays. Fifteen plays would be presented in the first season with Victor Mapes as dramatic director and Samuel P. Gerson as business manager. The owners hoped to give Chicago a theatrical company devoted to presenting the best stage plays. The entrance was enlarged, and the store to the east of the present entrance was remodeled and used as a box office and outer foyer.

The stage was enlarged with a fly loft, dressing rooms were added, and the seating capacity was enlarged to 850 roomy seats upholstered in a rose color with ten mezzanine boxes. Not just the aisles but the entire floor was carpeted. French gray, ivory, gold, and rose were the predominant colors used in the auditorium. A tearoom on the mezzanine floor served refreshments between acts, and a small stringed orchestra played during intermission. From the Van Buren Street entrance guests ascended a staircase to a small foyer spread with Turkish rugs, which opened immediately into the hall of the theatre.

On April 1, 1907, the New Theatre was reopened as the Whitney Opera House leased to Mr. B. C. Whitney. The auditorium remained the same with an orchestra pit added for musical comedy productions. Behind the curtain the changes were more apparent with the stage deepened some twelve feet. The Whitney Opera House opened with Smith-Hubbell's *A Knight for a Day*. In 1911, Sophie Tucker in *Mary, Mary* sang "I Used to Be a Widow; Now I'm a Kiddo."

Well-known actor Joe Howard opened Howard's Comedy Theatre on October 3, 1913, with the musical comedy *A Broadway Honeymoon*. Mr. Howard wrote the play and appeared in the production singing and dancing. Critics reported that there were a carload of flowers, a house full of people, and it was good to see "the old Whitney lighted up again" ("News of the Theaters," *Chicago Daily Tribune*, 4 October 1913).

On April 2, 1914, Selwyn and Company became the new proprietors of the theatre and renamed it the Comedy to present musical comedies. Alfred Hamburger secured the theatre as a movie house on September 13, 1914, with Universal's white slave feature *Traffic in Souls*, which had been showing at the Princess Theatre.

On March 26, 1915, the theatre became the Central Music Hall presenting a French farce. The theatre was used only intermittently by conventions and recitals. It was returned to a continuously lighted playhouse known as Shubert-Central reopening September 1, 1920, with *The Passion Flower*. In 1923, the playhouse became the Central Theatre with Owen Davis' *Up the Ladder*. Within a period of a few months, it was renamed Bryant's Central Theatre when Lester L. Bryant took over the lease, opening with another Owen Davis play, *Home Fires*. By September of 1924 the playhouse was called Bar-

rett's Central with Carl Barrett as owner. Within two months it was just the Central Theatre again with a series of comedies: *The Cat and the Canary* and *The Old Soak*. In 1926, the actor Harry Minturn took over the playhouse calling it the Minturn Central Theatre (William Leonard, "Wreckers Uncover Theater Nostalgia").

In 1929 construction started on the old Central Theatre to adapt it for the presentation of motion pictures. As the new lessee and manager, Louis Machat's vision for such a theatre was put in the hands of architect Eugene Fuhrer and theatre consultant Nicolas Remisoff (Remisoff, "The Punch and Judy Theatre").

The old theatre had a seating capacity of 850 for its presentations of light opera and musical productions, but in order to produce an intimate, modern theatre, seating capacity was reduced to 375. Specially designed chairs were installed similar to those in the Civic Opera House, as was a new ventilating system.

The Punch & Judy opened September 17, 1930, with D. W. Griffith's *Abraham Lincoln*. The biographical film about the American president starred Walter Huston as Lincoln and was the first feature-length talkie based on Lincoln's life. The film was the first of only two sound films made by Griffith and is now regarded as one of the definitive films about Lincoln. This was Griffith's second portrayal of Lincoln's assassination, the first done fifteen years earlier in *The Birth of a Nation*.

Renamed the Sonotone on March 21, 1935, the theatre was newly equipped for patrons who were hard of hearing and was managed by E. J. Stutz. This was said to be the first theatre in the world so equipped. Every seat was fitted with a device known as the Lieber Oscillator, which was furnished free of charge (some of the Balaban and Katz theatres had seats set aside in the rear where earphones could be plugged in on request) (Moore, "Totally Deaf Can Hear at This Theater").

The Punch & Judy introduced a new form for moving picture theatres, free from any kind of style and scenery.

On July 3, 1940, the theatre emerged as the Studio, with new management dedicated to public service and single, first-run features, newsreels and comedy shorts. *French without Tears* started off Studio's program. In 1952 the theatre was renamed the Ziegfeld, operated with Tom Dowd as manager until 1958 when Mr. Dowd became owner.

The newly redecorated "art" theatre, now renamed the Capri, opened on July 3,

Left: The upper balcony was incorporated into a domical ceiling and the other balcony converted into a loges. *Right:* The interior of the auditorium was transformed from a mostly square plan into more of a circular plan following the lines of the original balcony.

1958, with a controversial adult French film, *Nana*, based on an Emile Zola novel ("French Film to Open New Capri Theater Friday," *Chicago Tribune*, 29 June 1958). Adult films were shown until the theatre closed in 1968. The old theatre was torn down in June 1970.

1896 Clifford's Gaiety Theatre/
1900 Lyric Theatre

Clifford's Gaiety opened December 1, 1896, on the site of the old six-story stone Brunswick Billiard Hall on Washington Street between Clark and LaSalle Streets erected soon after the Great Fire. Next door was the Chicago Opera House and opposite on Washington Street was the old city hall. Under the direction of manager David Henderson, the attractions at the new theatre consisted of light opera, extravaganzas, and "burlesque of the best order." The opening performance was *LaFille de Mme. Angot*, an opera comique.

The theatre was like no other in that its style resembled a French or German theatre. There were thirty-four boxes, lounging rooms, cafes and a buffet that were connected with the house behind the first balcony "so one could keep an eye on the performance." The balcony was known as the dress circle. A performance was held every night including Sunday, with matinees on Wednesday and Saturday. Veriscope pictures of the Fitzsimmons-Corbett fight broke attendance records on June 20, 1897. Mr. Clifford closed the theatre in 1899.

Remodeled and renamed the Lyric, the theatre was reopened on March 8, 1900, by Martin Julian. The theatre joined the "10–20–30" vaudeville ranks, presenting plays on occasion. On November 12, 1900, the interior of the playhouse was destroyed by a fire. Crossed electric wires were reported to have been the cause of the disaster. The theatre never reopened.

1898 Studebaker Theatre/1899 Music Hall/1912 Fine Arts Theatre/1916 Playhouse/1933 World Playhouse/ 1982 Fine Arts Theatres

The Studebaker Building at 410 South Michigan Avenue was built in 1885 in a Romanesque style, designed by Solon S. Beman as a showroom and assembly plant for the Studebaker Carriage Company, makers of horse-drawn carriages and wagons. The first few floors of the eight-story building near Van Buren Street were originally showrooms for carriages, with the manufacturing functions on the floors above. (The company ultimately designed and manufactured automobiles, moving their facility to South Bend, Indiana.) In 1898, renamed the Fine Arts Building when Studebaker moved, the building became known as the Carnegie Hall of Chicago. The first floor provided theatre space, while the rest of the building housed the offices of music, art, and drama teachers, including those of L. Frank Baum, Lorado Taft, and Frank Lloyd Wright. Remodeled by the original architect, the original top floor was replaced with three more floors to be used as artists' and musicians' studios. The upper-floor studios overlooked Lake Front (now Grant) Park and Lake Michigan.

Within the newly renovated building, the larger of two ground-floor music halls with approximately 1,000 seats was transformed into the Studebaker Theatre and opened on September 29, 1898, presenting the popular stage presentations of the time. The Victorian design featured a three-tier auditorium with thirty-two boxes and outstanding acoustics. The Studebaker closed for the month of August 1907 for a "thorough overhauling" and opened the new season with George Ade's play *Artie*, a dramatization of a well-known book.

The smaller hall of approximately 450 seats, with its entrance at the opposite end of the lobby, opened on December 29, 1899, as University Hall/Music Hall presenting music performances and lectures. On October 1,

View from the lounge toward stair foyer. A coffee bar was on the left (Punch & Judy Theatre).

1912, the Music Hall, renamed the Fine Arts Theatre, opened the occasion with a program of songs. In 1913 the Chicago Theatre Society Repertory Company presented plays. From May 16, 1914, the theatre became part of the Alfred Hamburger theatre circuit. The latest bulletins from the war front in the form of moving pictures were shown, along with popular photoplays. Again, the theatre was renamed the Playhouse on November 20, 1916. *Chicago Tribune* advertisements called it "Chicago's Daintiest Theatre" (28 September 1919). Concerts and recitals were also presented, namely, the farewell concert of the Flonzaley String Quartet on March 3, 1929.

On April 30, 1933, the theatre, now renamed the World Playhouse, opened with the musical comedy *Be Mine Tonight*. During the 1933 World's Fair it was a premier location to see moving pictures and became a popular venue for art and foreign films in Chicago, lasting until 1972. The World Playhouse was the first theatre in the Midwest to play films such as *The Bicycle Thief*, and the first Chicago showing of films by Ingmar

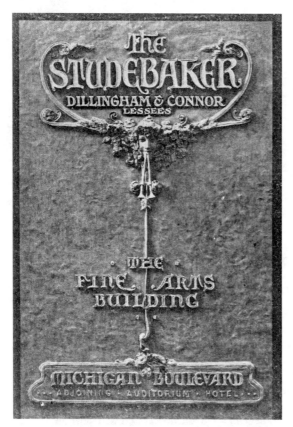 

Left: The first week of June 1907 Charles Dillingham and W. F. Connor leased the Studebaker and promised first-rate entertainment for playgoers. *Right:* The Studebaker interior window detail, circa 1920.

Bergman. When the theatre celebrated its twentieth anniversary, it marked the occasion with the French film *Forbidden Games*. In 1953 it was the "sole outlet for imports" (Tinee, "Movies"). Eventually reduced to showing X-rated material, the World Playhouse closed on February 10, 1972.

After sitting deserted and in disrepair for eight years, the World Playhouse reopened on October 20, 1980, with a new curtain, stage floor, and dressing rooms for the Fine Art Quartet to begin their twenty-first season in the acoustically excellent theatre (Christiansen, "World Playhouse Ready to Return to Arts Action").

The Studebaker Theatre with Louis J. Jones as manager and part of the Jones, Linick and Schaefer theatre circuit advertised its first moving picture on November 14, 1914, *On Belgian Battlefields in the Great European*

War. The four reels of film were shot by Edwin F. Weigle of the *Chicago Tribune*, the first authentic motion pictures of the war. Pictures from Japan with a lecture shown on May 17, 1915, were said to be extremely clear, steadily projected and told with human interest. A pipe organ supplied musical accompaniment. During December of 1916, William Fox's film spectacle, a moving picture of novelty and sensation, *The Daughter of the Gods*, was presented twice daily.

When the theatre failed to turn a profit, it was remodeled again into a legitimate theatre for the Shubert Organization, reopening on November 5, 1917. Designed by Andrew N. Rebori, the theatre now featured an enlarged stage, new lighting facilities, and improved acoustics. On August 6, 1934, *The Mikado* started a season of revivals of Gilbert and Sullivan comic operas. In April 1943,

Auditorium of the Studebaker Theatre with right side wall.

under the management of Frank McCoy, *Stage Door* was the first in a series of presentations to continue during that wartime summer (Smith, "Play First of Popular Priced Attractions Planned for City").

After *Light Up the Sky* closed on February 11, 1950, the Studebaker closed for six years, to be converted into a television studio to accommodate the "Chicago School of Television." In October 1956 it was restored to live drama with a season of resident repertory. In late summer of 1968 (11 August), noted *Chicago Tribune* columnist William Leonard wrote that a theatre tragedy may once again be imminent with the possibility of the Studebaker being turned once again into a movie theatre. "It could be the beginning of the end of Chicago as a theatre town."

The Studebaker Theatre closed in 1978,

the year that the Fine Arts Building was designated a Chicago Landmark. In 1975 the Fine Arts Building had been placed on the National Register of Historic Places.

On Christmas Day 1982, M&R Amusements began operating the Studebaker Theatre and World Playhouse as Fine Arts 1 (Studebaker) and 2 (World Playhouse), showing *Moonlighting* in 1 and Fassbinder's *Veronika Voss* in 2. By Christmas 1983, a third screen was added to the Fine Arts with 300 seats (Siskel, "M&R Will Add Third Screen to Fine Arts").

By 1984 a four-screen complex was achieved by building a wall over the prosceniums, making two large movie houses of 500 seats each where the auditoriums were and two smaller spaces on the actual stages. The Fine Arts 4, the smaller of the two new screens, seating only 158, was particularly

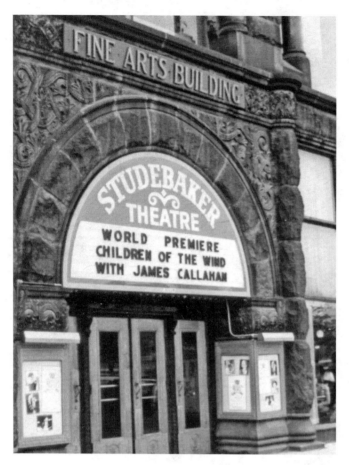

well designed (Siskel, "Rating the New Multiplexes"). For much of the 1980s, the Fine Arts was the place to see the top first-run foreign-language and independent films. When M&R merged with Loews Cineplex Entertainment in 1988, programming began to deteriorate along with the theatres. November 29, 2000, marked the close of the Fine Arts Theatres.

In 2008, Fine Arts Building owner Robert Berger commissioned prominent theatre architect Daniel P. Coffey to prepare a "plan for the rehabilitation of the two historic theater spaces contained within this landmark structure" (Jones, "Chicago's Fine Arts Building").

The Jerry Devine play *Children of the Wind* set in the 1930s premiered at the Studebaker Theatre in 1973.

Theatres Opening from 1900

Playhouses flourished at the turn of the century. Chicago had held the World's Columbian Exposition introducing the public to buildings of a new kind of architecture. The amusement arcades on the Midway featured moving images on individually viewed peep-show machines. And before the first moving picture theatres opened on State Street, these moving images were presented in several of downtown's popular playhouses.

1900 Illinois Theatre

The Illinois Theatre was built to assume the bookings of the Columbia Theatre, which had been destroyed by fire. At 61–65 East Jackson Street, the theatre was designed by Benjamin Marshall in the Beaux-Arts style, inspired by the buildings of the World's Columbian Exposition of 1893.

The opening of the theatre was a spectacular event on October 15, 1900, with Julia Marlowe staring in *Barbara Frietchie*. The Illinois Theatre was the first monumental structure of its kind in America, devoted to theatrical purposes only. Entirely built of stone with the first story of polished granite, the three-story facade featured a row of Ionic columns above the main entrance. The theatre's name was inscribed just below the cornice in large letters. The entrances were spacious with fourteen doors. The walls of the entrance lobby were of Carrara marble inlaid with turquoise blue. The ceiling of this lobby was thirty-five feet high. The decorations for the interior were in the style of Louis XIV primarily using the color rose with gilded and burnished woodwork. The proscenium arch had elaborate ornamentation inlaid with mother-of-pearl. The ventilation of this 1,287-seat theatre was given special attention and was helped by its being an isolated building ("Illinois Theater to Be Ready for Opening on Oct. 1," *Chicago Daily Tribune*, 16 January 1900).

The Illinois Theatre was one the city's leading downtown playhouses for big musical extravaganzas. It became the home of the Ziegfeld Follies and was managed by Rollo Timponi. There was a separate entrance from the street to accommodate the increasing number of women who went to the theatre.

The theatre had been under construction since the early spring on the old Armory lot, formerly home to the headquarters of the First Regiment. The building was owned by Will J. Davis and Harry J. Powers of Chicago with Al Hayman, Charles Frohman, Marcus Klaw and A. L. Erlanger of New York. Messrs. Hayman and Davis managed the theatre. Harry J. Powers, the veteran theatre man, booked many famous dramas for four decades in the Illinois.

In July 1915, D. W. Griffith's *Birth of a Nation* was in its second record month at the Illinois fueled by its controversial racist material. The film is recognized by film scholars as a key film in movie history for its new cinematic innovations and technical effects. During the 1920s, moving pictures became the featured presentation at the Illinois. A new D. W. Griffith comic mystery, *One Exciting Night*, presented in 1922, was very well reviewed (Butler, "Theater Notes").

During the Depression in 1934, the theatre closed never to reopen. On January 15, 1936, the demolition of the historic theatre

began for "an open air parking station" (Chase, "Final Curtain Falls for Old Illinois Theater").

1902 LaSalle Theatre

The LaSalle Theatre at 110 West Madison Street near Clark Street opened on December 21, 1902. Designed in the popular Beaux-Arts style, the two-story building fronted eighty feet on Madison. New ordinances enacted after the Iroquois fire closed the LaSalle Theatre and required that seating be reduced to less than 600 seats before it reopened as a class 4 building on February 21, 1904. The seating was reduced by cutting a cross aisle leading directly to the main entrance, and by taking out some of the side seats. Being an upstairs house, the LaSalle could not use a steel curtain as others were required to install. Therefore, to comply with the ordinances, the scenery was painted on sheet iron. When the LaSalle Theatre reopened, the *Belle of Newport* was applauded by the audience that packed the house.

Operas, musical comedy, legitimate theatre, and vaudeville acts were presented, but the LaSalle Theatre gained renown as the birthplace of musical comedy. For many years most of the popular lighter musical plays originated and were produced at the LaSalle Theatre. In July of 1908, Manager Mort Singer announced renovation plans to make the LaSalle more like his Princess Theatre. One added feature was a lounging parlor in what used to be the lobby.

The theatre was rebuilt in 1913 to exit at street level. Jones, Linick and Schaefer became the owners of the LaSalle Theatre on August 24, 1913, and named Harry Earl as manager of the theatre. *September Morn* remained the attraction on stage. The theatre showed movies throughout the summer of 1915, beginning on July 19 with Essanay's six-reel feature film *The Blindness of Virtue*. On December 5, 1915, the theatre exhibited for the first time in Chicago the official motion pictures obtained by the *Chicago American* taken under the authorization of the governments in France, Russia, Italy, and Serbia. These pictures showed the Allies in action, in actual battle. The LaSalle became a motion picture theatre from May 1927 when James Roder, who operated the Astor Theatre, signed the lease to take over the LaSalle with continuous performances from 9:00 A.M. to 11:00 P.M. The first moving picture was Mary Pickford in *The Pride of the Clan*.

The Franciscan Fathers Roman Catholic order desired to build a new church and monastery in the heart of the Loop and purchased the LaSalle Theatre property on July 11, 1949. Simultaneously, the Franciscan Fathers sold their ten-story Woods Theatre Building to the Woods Amusement Corporation, a subsidiary of Essaness Theatres Cor-

poration. The new building replaced the old St. Peter's Church (1875) at the southwest corner of Clark and Polk streets, in continuous use since it was built ("Catholic Order Pays $515,000 for Loop Suite," *Chicago Daily Tribune*, 12 July 1949).

1903 Iroquois Theatre/
1904 Hyde & Behman's Music Hall/
1905 Colonial Theatre

The six-story Iroquois Theatre at 24–28 West Randolph Street opened on November 23, 1903, designed in the Beaux-Arts style made popular by the 1893 World's Columbian Exposition in Chicago. The architect, Benjamin Marshall, also had designed the Illinois Theatre and remodeled the Powers' Theatre. The Iroquois with 1,724 seats was advertised as "absolutely fireproof," equipped with an asbestos curtain that could be lowered to separate the audience from any fire on stage.

The Iroquois was filled with a standing-room-only crowd of 1,900 for the matinee performance on December 30 of the musical *Mr. Bluebeard*. The vaudeville comedian Eddie Foy was on stage when at the start of the second act, painted canvas scenery above the stage, too close to a spotlight, caught on fire. The fire spread quickly. The theatre's asbestos curtain jammed on the way down.

In a panic, those on stage rushed out a stage door at the rear of the theatre letting in a blast of air, which only fed the flames more. The fire jumped into the auditorium and quickly reached the second and third levels. As the stage began to collapse, people rushed for the twenty-seven exits. But

The LaSalle Theatre just before closing in 1949.

The Iroquois Theatre was described as a magnificent palace of marble and mahogany, "a virtual temple of beauty."

some of the exits were locked. Others opened inward. People jumped from the upper levels to escape the spreading flames. In this fire, 602 people died, making it the worst disaster in Chicago's history — a greater death toll than the Great Chicago Fire of 1871. It is also considered the deadliest single-building fire in U.S. history.

The fire led to tougher safety standards nationwide. In Chicago, Mayor Carter H.

Top: Playbill for the new Colonial Theatre. *Bottom:* "The Theatre Beautiful."

Harrison shut down theatres, halls and churches for a six-week-long reinspection. New laws were enacted to change the fire code to require theatre doors to open outwards, to have exits clearly marked, fire curtains made of steel, and a new limit of six or eight on the maximum number of seats between aisles (for faster evacuation) (Brandt, Duis, and Schallhorn, *Chicago Death Trap*).

The management of the Iroquois wanted to reopen the theatre, now referred to as "the Hall of Death" in the newspapers. The exterior of the theatre remained largely intact. Two hundred and sixty-three days after the fire, the Iroquois was reopened, now called Hyde & Behman's Music Hall. Louis Behman and his schoolmate Richard Hyde had opened their first theatre in Brooklyn, New York. Their Chicago theatre was devoted to vaudeville with Archie Ellis as manager ("Iroquois Is Open," *Chicago Daily Tribune*, 2 September 1904). "Matinee Every Day" was part of Hyde & Behman's ads in the *Chicago Daily Tribune*. A change in policy was announced to begin February 6, 1905. Vaudeville was discontinued and dramas were presented (*Chicago Daily Tribune*, 24 January 1905). However, before the theatre went dark for the 1905 summer season, vaudeville was again featured. These were to be Hyde & Behman's last shows ("Playbills," *Chicago Daily Tribune*, 16 June 1905).

The theatre was rebuilt and reopened as the Colonial on September 22, 1905, with a new musical play by George M. Cohan, *Forty-five Minutes from Broadway*, starring Fay Templeton. George W. Lederer, formerly with Hyde & Behman's, assumed management of the new theatre. Klaw and Erlanger supplied the theatre with its attractions. The theatre became the home of musical comedy and in later years featured the Ziegfeld Follies and the Music Box Review when Harry J. Powers was owner with James J. Brady as manager.

On May 27, 1913, Percy Hammond, theatre critic of the *Chicago Daily Tribune*, wrote a long review about this handsome theatre's shift from a policy of musical comedy to vaudeville, now under the management of Jones, Linick and Schaefer "who sell their wares at 25 cents instead of 75 cents for the best seats." Norman E. Field who had been Jones, Linick and Schaefer's manager in their first Chicago movie theatre initiated a policy of feature pictures for the summer months. In May of 1915, *Birth of a Nation* was on the screen, and on July 22, 1916, Chicagoans saw for the first time *The German Side of the War*. Edwin F. Weigle, staff war photographer of the *Chicago Tribune*, appeared in each of six reels ("New German War Films Tomorrow," *Chicago Daily Tribune*, 21 July 1916). The Colonial Theatre closed its doors on May 17, 1924, to be torn down to make way for a new nineteen-story United Masonic Building. The

This was the first permanent home owned by any major American symphony orchestra.

work of tearing down the building was to begin the following week ("Rialto Loses a Landmark," *Chicago Daily Tribune*, 18 May 1924).

1904 Orchestra Hall

Daniel H. Burnham designed Orchestra Hall at 220 South Michigan Avenue in a Beaux-Arts style specifically as the permanent home of the Chicago Symphony Orchestra. The first music director, Theodore Thomas, led the orchestra in the first dedicatory concert held on December 14, 1904. All 2,581 seats were filled.

In order to boost revenues during the summer months, the Orchestra Association decided, in the summer of 1913, to rent the hall to show the new moving pictures and installed a temporary marquee on the building. *Les Miserables* was so popular it was shown throughout the summer, closing in October of 1913. On May 1, 1915, the Strand Theatre Company took over management of the newly furnished hall introducing a "new venture of pictures with trimmings." Lasky's production of *The Woman* was presented along with a concert (Kelly, "Chicagoans See Novel Film Show"). In 1924, Orchestra Hall was under the management of Lubliner and Trinz. In the 1940s, in response to the spread of war in Europe, civic groups rented Orchestra Hall to sponsor benefit programs.

Daniel Burnham Jr. was responsible for the first renovation in 1950. Renovations occurred in 1966 and from 1993 to 1997 with

At times during the 1920s and 1930s the stage was used for lectures by prominent persons.

the main agenda being to improve the acoustics. Listed on the National Register of Historic Places in 1978, Orchestra Hall is now called Symphony Center.

1906 Majestic Theatre/ 1945 Shubert Theatre

The Majestic Theatre at 18 West Monroe Street opened on January 1, 1906, for vaudeville. The eight Allisons, a family of acrobats, headed the opening bill.

Construction lasted eighteen months and adhered to Chicago's new building laws governing places of amusement (W. L. Hubbard, "News of the Theaters"). Designed by Edmund R. Krause aided by the young Rapp

brothers, the Majestic was the first theatre built after the Iroquois Theatre fire, and the first venue in Chicago to cost over one million dollars.

The seating capacity of 2,000 included the lower floor, mezzanine, balcony, and gallery. The only playhouse larger in seating capacity was the Auditorium. The new mezzanine consisted of a shallow balcony immediately over the back of the parquet. The arrangement provided for thirty private boxes and combined with the twenty-four proscenium loges gave the theatre the unusual total of fifty-four boxes. The mezzanine and balcony were brought far enough forward to make the stage seem close at hand.

Old gold and ivory were used on all the

At the time, the Majestic building was one of the tallest buildings in Chicago.

elaborate plaster work which faced the proscenium arch, and old rose covered the walls. The color scheme of the foyer on the lower floor was old rose, soft gray, and olive green with the stairways of marble.

Sarah Bernhardt appeared on the stage of the Majestic Theatre in December of 1912. Ethel Barrymore was on stage two years later. In 1913, Edison demonstrated his talking pictures invention at the Majestic. In December

Becoming one of the most successful vaudeville houses in the country, the Majestic ran twelve to fifteen "high-class vaudeville" acts continuously.

of that year the variety acts presented included moving pictures of Fred and Irene Castle dancing. The Castles were filmed in their New York studio, the first such successful representation. The Majestic became part of the Orpheum Circuit in the early 1920s, but when vaudeville began to lose its popularity, melodrama and legitimate stage productions were featured on the stage.

A first-release feature picture was shown on September 25, 1927, in conjunction with its vaudeville presentation as was the policy at the State-Lake Theatre. The first feature was *Jaws of Steel* starring the dog star Rin-Tin-Tin (Tinee, "Another Star Portrayal Given by Rin-Tin-Tin"). On October 20, 1931, the Shubert Theater Corporation was placed in equity receivership due to a decline

in attendance with no reduction in operating costs since the stock market crash of 1929. (In addition to the Majestic, the Shubert interests at that time included the Selwyn, Harris, Garrick, Apollo, Grand Opera House, Great Northern, and Princess theatres.) On March 15, 1934, Jones, Linick and Schaefer leased the Majestic with Aaron Jones as manager. At the end of that year, Jones, Linick and Schaefer still operated three other Loop playhouses, the State-Lake, Woods, and Rialto theatres, when the Majestic Theatre went dark for eleven years.

The theatre reopened on September 18, 1945, remodeled and renamed the Shubert for its new owners, a legitimate theatre featuring Broadway shows. This added a ninth theatre to the number of major playhouses

Four tiers of boxes still flanked the broad stage. The mezzanine floor surmounted by two balconies could now be accessed by elevators.

downtown, and one of the largest legitimate houses. Olson and Johnson's musical revue, *Laffing Room Only*, opened the new theatre with Illinois governor Green and Chicago mayor Kelly in attendance. The spaciousness of the earlier theatre remained in the wide lobbies, marble staircases, and glittering chandeliers. Rose and gold were selected as the new colors for the auditorium.

In 1991 the Shubert Organization sold the theatre to the Nederlander Organization. Since 2000 the theatre has been owned and operated by Broadway in Chicago and host to pre–Broadway productions and world premieres (Abarbanel, "Shubert Goes Back to the Future"). Between January 2005 and May 2006 the theatre underwent a restoration

with naming rights sold to the LaSalle Bank. The lobbies were doubled in size, and the false ceiling that was put up over the outer lobby years ago was removed to reveal the original two-story atrium. The original mosaic floor installed in the lobby when the theatre opened and most of the original fixtures remain. Elevators were installed within the theatre. The lower-level restrooms were enlarged, the interior was restored to its original color scheme, and the seats were replaced. The 2,016 seats included the orchestra level, loge, mezzanine, balcony and side boxes.

There was a new marquee for the LaSalle Bank Theatre; the bottom of the canopy is modeled after the original metal that had been left in place for years, exposed during

the renovation. The theatre was renamed the Bank of America Theatre in May 2008 when the LaSalle Bank organization was acquired by Bank of America.

1906 Hale's Tours and Scenes of the World

The penny arcade that had been on State Street just south of Monroe Street across the street from the Palmer House was remodeled to resemble two rear observation train platforms. There was a sign that read "Trains Every 10 Minutes." The entrance to the "theatre" was through the observation platform. When seated you might see "flickers" of the Rocky Mountains or rickshaws in the streets of a town in China as you sped along the railroad track. Sometimes a whistle blew, sometimes a bell rang, and always the "coach" in which you were riding would be shaking like a real train. You paid a dime and could travel to Africa, India, or Russia.

Hale's Tours was a nickelodeon amusement invented by Kansas City fire chief George C. Hale. It was an "illusion ride" composed of train cars that each seated seventy-two "passengers." The pictures depicting scenes from around the world were seven to ten minutes long (Wagenknecht, "When Movies Cost Five Cents, Lasted 30 Minutes"). Hale's Tours remained open until Jones, Linick & Schaefer built their Orpheum Theatre on the site.

1907 Orpheum Theatre

Advertising "continuous vaudeville" inscribed on the arch of the facade, the Orpheum Theatre at 110–112 South State Street opened on October 9, 1907. Built for the "nickel kings" in the Beaux-Arts style, a stylized peacock in the center over the archway was illuminated by electric lights. The white terra cotta facade resembled marble. However, when it was built, every theatre manager predicted it would not be successful because of the theatrical superstition regarding the peacock as a bad omen (Neil G. Caward, "The Rise of Jones, Linick & Schaefer").

The interior of the Orpheum was two stories high decorated in the style of a late nineteenth-century opera house. There was a small balcony, a double aisle on the main floor, plush seats, and several opera boxes. Theatre organs were installed in 1909 and 1912. This was Jones, Linick and Schaefer's first great success: the only "First Run Daily Change" moving picture house in Chicago. The performances were continuous from eight in the morning to midnight.

The Orpheum started showing movies interspersed with sing-along slide shows in 1909 when it dropped vaudeville and became a movie house. Originally the Orpheum showed several short reels for an admission fee of five cents; then Jones, Linick and Schaefer decided to raise the price of admission to ten cents in 1912. The first feature picture was *Judith of Bethulia*, which critics say marked the start of real drama in the flickers. The Orpheum was the first Chicago moving picture theatre to charge more than a nickel and the first to show features consisting of two reels. In 1913, Jones, Linick and Schaefer completed the installation of a "mirror screen" consisting of one solid sheet of glass fourteen feet wide and eighteen feet high. Patrons commented on the improvement in the pictures shown (*Inter Ocean Morning News*, 2 March 1913).

On June 29, 1925, Warner Bros. Pictures subleased the Orpheum from Jones, Linick and Schaefer to premier their movies (Al Chase, "Warner Bros. Lease Orpheum From "J. L. & S."").

The Vitaphone system was Warner's sound-on-disc system, which in collaboration with Western Electric and Bell Labs in 1926 presented the first successful commer-

Opposite top: The 1963 Tony Award-winning musical *Oliver* appeared direct from the Broadway stage. *Opposite bottom:* The Bank of America Theatre in 2010. (Photograph by the author.)

cial sound picture, *Don Juan*, with John Barrymore. This first feature-length movie with a synchronized musical background and a prerecorded score premiered at the Orpheum on February 18, 1927. With a seating capacity of 799, the Orpheum premiered many early sound pictures.

On April 28, 1937, the Orpheum closed, running an "adults only" feature. "The theatre will be torn out and the basement and first and second floors completely remodeled into an air-conditioned, modern shoe shop" (Chase, "Oldest Chicago Loop Cinema to Close Doors"). Kitty Kelly Shoes opened their first Chicago store on September 8, 1937.

1907 Bijou Dream Theatre

The Bijou Dream Theatre at 114 South State Street near Monroe Street was next door to the Orpheum. An early holding of the Jones, Linick and Schaefer circuit, the theatre opened on May 1, 1907, with Sigmund Faller as manager. The Bijou Dream presented a vaudeville show for ten cents on the first floor. Three acts were presented from 10 A.M. to 5 P.M., while another shift relieved until midnight. Moving pictures could be seen on the second floor for five cents, with the screen at the front of the building. To reach the 296-seat theatre, you climbed a glass staircase with a waterfall underneath, illuminated by colored electric lights.

Top: The Orpheum was considered one of the most beautiful theatre facades in Chicago. *Bottom:* Flags were strung across State Street to celebrate Memorial Day 1926; the Orpheum was playing Cecil B. DeMille's *The Volga Boatman.*

A large marquee was added to the Orpheum's facade for Warner's Vitaphone system.

By 1915 the Bijou Dream would be the home of feature pictures. The theatre closed in August of 1922. The Bijou Dream was purchased in 1925 and converted into the sixth DeMet's candy store in the Loop.

1907 Lyric Theatre

Built specifically for showing moving pictures, the Lyric Theatre opened on June 15, 1907, another Jones, Linick and Schaefer theatre. At 348 South State Street near Van Buren Street, the theatre was managed by Louis J. Jones and was closed a short time in 1911 for remodeling. When it reopened, the two upper floors of the building had been removed to make room for a balcony. The seating capacity was increased by 150 making the seating capacity of the house nearly 500. The

"operating room" (room for the projectors) had been placed at the top of the new balcony. The mirror screen was still in place providing a clearer picture on screen. Under the balcony three indirect lighting fixtures were installed to light the theater, while the balcony itself effectively protected the screen from the light ("Chicago Picture Shows," *Moving Picture World*, 29 July 1911).

The Lyric Theatre was in a class by itself at the time, being the only twenty-four-hour theatre in the world. Three shifts of employees presented moving pictures every twenty-four hours out of every day, 365 days every year. Renamed the Strand in 1915, the theatre remained open for only a few months.

A new Lyric with 286 seats was opened at 320 South State Street in 1916, also owned by Jones, Linick and Schaefer. This Lyric closed in 1921.

The Bijou Dream presented vaudeville, moving pictures, and illustrated songs. The facade was courtesy of the Decorators Supply Company.

1907 Alcazar Theatre

The Alcazar was the oldest theatre on the street opening in May 1907 at 69 West Madison Street. (Early documents give the address as 108 Madison.) The theatre was built by Harry C. Moir, owner of the Morrison Hotel near Chicago's first Theatre Row at the intersection of Madison and Clark streets (*The Film Index*, 20 August 1910).

The frontage of the Alcazar Theatre was twenty-one feet wide, typical of the early five-cent movie theatres. Movie banners were usually stretched across the front of the theatre blocking much of the archway while cherubs sat on top of the facade. In December 1908, a Hinners organ was installed making it the first picture show with an organ in downtown Chicago. A piano and drum were also installed. A. H. Talbot, manager of the Alcazar, featured moving pictures until nearby competing houses introduced vaudeville.

The organ was to the left of the screen, with its pipe grills on the front left and right walls. The 300 seats were all wooden. The Alcazar was running as an all-night movie house in its last years and closed in 1929 as part of the Jones, Linick and Schaefer circuit.

1908 Boston Theatre

The Boston Theatre at 79 West Madison Street (early documents give the address as 114 Madison) was one of the three early theatres owned by Harry C. Moir, owner of the Morrison Hotel. James W. Ferris was manager from the theatre's opening and was in favor

The interior of the Alcazar theatre in 1909 was typical of the first nickelodeons having just a center aisle.

of exclusive picture entertainment. Fourteen reels of film were used a week, five first runs, with the George K. Spoor Company attending to the film bookings. In 1910, there were two acts of vaudeville daily and one act of illustrated songs.

In 1912, the Boston Theatre was closed and razed to make way for the first expansion of the hotel, which was designed by Marshall and Fox.

Moir built a (new) Boston theatre in 1912 at 21 North Clark Street, with 400 seats, next to the Columbia Theatre.

Harry C. Moir was the owner of the Morrison Hotel, the first of which was eight stories high and was started in 1883 at 71–89 West Madison Street. It was replaced in 1914 with a twenty-three story building designed by architects Marshall & Fox.

In 1925 the Morrison Hotel Tower,

forty-five stories, was built adjoining at 15–29 South Clark Street. The new tower, completed in 1927, added 400 new rooms and raised the height of the building to 46 stories above street level making it one of the tallest buildings in Chicago, and the largest hotel west of New York in the 1920s.

Mr. Moir lost the property in the early 1930s to the First National Bank, who demolished the building in 1965 to make room for the First National Bank Building, now Chase Tower.

1908 Pastime Theatre/ 1941 Today Theatre

The Pastime Theatre opened opposite the Alcazar Theatre on the south side of the street at 66 West Madison Street. (Early documents give the address as 109 Madison.) F.

The theatre was adjacent to the Boston Oyster House, a landmark restaurant in downtown Chicago in the Morrison Hotel.

C. Aiken was manager of the theatre and arranged with the managers of the Casino Garden and Alcazar theatres to present vaudeville only on Saturdays and Sundays during the summer of 1910. Films by the General Film Company were booked and could be selected to prevent any conflict with those shown at other theatres.

The theatre had a frontage of twenty feet wide with a depth of 190 feet, and a seating capacity of 460. The balcony boxes were equally divided into one for ladies, one for

The auditorium of the renovated Today.

men. The Pastime had the largest projection in the Loop giving a picture 15¾ × 13½ feet (McQuade, "Picture Row").

New house manager E. J. Barrett used extensive posters and signs for the two reels of moving pictures presented daily. High-class vaudeville and a character singer or illustrated songs comprised the bill for ten cents. The Pastime closed in September 1939.

March 1, 1941, marked the opening of the theatre renamed the Today devoted to showing newsreels. The owner, Richard Beck, had engaged industrial designer David Chapman "to create as fine a small theatre as was possible." The seating capacity was now 327 with continuous one-hour shows of newsreels and short subjects, one of only two theatres in the Loop showing the latest news. After the theatre was shut down by the city for violations along with five other theatres, the Today closed in 1975 and was razed three years later.

1908 Princess Theatre

Opening on June 1, 1908, Mort H. Singer's new playhouse at 317–321 South Clark Street was built on a lot 75 feet wide and 110 feet deep. Mr. Singer continued his management of the LaSalle Theatre at this time. The exterior of the theatre was of white terra cotta with a roof of red tile. The entire lobby and stairways were of marble. Stairs on the left led to the balcony; the box office was on the right. The theatre was constructed with twenty-two exits and four wide steel and concrete safety tunnels, all leading directly into the street or a wide alley.

A feature of the theatre was its ventilation system. The air in the theatre was changed every three minutes, drawn through cloths to be purified as it was brought in. It was then, depending on the weather, run through a series of pipes to be either cooled or heated.

This early premier Loop playhouse,

Two great double doors exactly centered opened into the lobby.

"devoted exclusively to theatrical purposes," had a seating capacity of 982, which included the balcony, boxes, and loges ("New Playhouse for Clark Street," *Chicago Daily Tribune*, 9 November 1907).

The Princess Theatre opened with a musical comedy by Adams and Hough, *A Stubborn Cinderella*, with music by Joe Howard. A very young John Barrymore was leading man. The opening attraction ran for ten months. The Princess was known for its Chicago productions of musical comedies and later became the home of many well-known dramas when the Shuberts leased the theatre.

The Princess featured the six-reel feature *Uncle Tom's Cabin* on August 8, 1914. On April 16, 1933, the Princess reopened after three years of idleness to present the detective comedy *Riddle Me This*. The latest "Soviet Talkie with English Dialog," *Frontier*, was listed in the *Chicago Daily Tribune* at the Princess from June 10, 1936.

This early playhouse closed in 1937, having shown pictures intermittently, and was demolished in 1941 for a parking lot. Both the Illinois and Cort theatres had closed in 1934 ("Famed Old Princess Theatre Yields to the Ax of Wreckers," *Chicago Daily Tribune*, 12 July 1941).

1909 Cort Theatre

In the heart of the Rialto, the Cort Theatre at 126–132 North Dearborn Street opened on October 25, 1909, with the first Chicago performance of the comic opera *The Kissing Girl*.

Designed by J.E.O. Pridmore, the early atmospheric effects in the Cort Theatre would become the forerunner for later such theatres in Chicago. This short, steep little playhouse had a ceiling representing a night sky with twinkling stars. The design was Italian rustic with a panorama painting on the curtain of an ancient Greek theatre in Sicily.

Fluted columns with Corinthian capitals flanked the proscenium arch. The boxes on the sides were arranged in an unusual stair-step fashion. A mezzanine floor with loges was under the first balcony. Above everything was a Roman pergola of vine-clad beams and lattice said to have been identical to those in the old Taormina Theatre, which served Pridmore as a model. Ivory and green were the prominent colors. The Cort was small so that everyone could see and hear the productions on stage, which were mostly domestic comedies ("Play and Playhouse Scored Successes," *Chicago Daily Tribune*, 26 October 1909).

March 22, 1931, marked the reopening of the Cort after being closed for a year. A new comedy, *When Father Smiles*, premiered. However,

By 1912 the Princess Theatre (as well as the Garrick and Lyric) were Shubert houses.

owner and manager Urban J. "Sport" Herrmann announced in 1934 that he could no longer operate the theatre under the old policy and he would not "surrender to showing movies" (Collins, "Cort Theatre Surrenders to Drama Famine"). Mr. Herrmann considered remodeling the Cort into a theatre restaurant or a supper club. The Cort Theatre's last performance was October 2, 1934. The building was eventually razed and the site used for parking.

1909 Ziegfeld Theatre

Christian A. Ecksrom designed the eight-story brick building in 1908 at 624 South Michigan Avenue. The building, faced with Bedford limestone on its first two floors, was commissioned by Dr. Florenz Ziegfeld Sr. to house his Chicago Musical College. (His son became the producer of the famous Ziegfeld Follies.) The Chicago Academy of Music had been housed in the Crosby Opera House before the Great Fire. In 1872, Dr.

Ziegfeld's music academy was on South Wabash Avenue near Van Buren Street.

Chicago's new lakefront theatre, named after Dr. Ziegfeld, was housed on the ground floor. The floors were mosaic, the woodwork mahogany, and Italian marble was used for the walls and groined ceiling. The theatre

The building is now part of the Historic Michigan Boulevard Landmark District.

opened in October of 1909. In December of that year the Vienna Opera Company presented the light opera *The Mousetrap Peddler*.

When the Alfred Hamburger theatre circuit acquired the "Ziegfeld Picture Playhouse," as they called it, a full-page ad appeared in the *Chicago Tribune* on January 10, 1914. Opening in six parts was the photoplay

Richard Wagner's Life Drama with all seats costing twenty-five cents. There were two performances in the afternoon and two in the evening, daily and Sundays. In December 1915, Mae Tinee, movie critic for the *Chicago Tribune*, wrote that the Ziegfeld was no longer a movie house but a "picture theatre."

Its double feature programs were embellished with orchestral accompaniment, and programs were provided to patrons. It was advertised as the "Coolest Theatre in the City."

For a brief time Hamburger renamed the theatre the V.L.S.E. Theatre in 1916 for the Vitagraph, Lubin, Selig, Essanay moving picture studios that were part of a cooperative distribution agreement. In 1918, the Ziegfeld was the only theatre in the city to feature Douglas Fairbanks in *Mr. Fix-It* for an admission price of twenty-five cents. In 1919, the theatre was leased by Linick-Jacoby Enterprises. D. W. Griffith's 1921 film *Dream Street* ran for fourteen weeks, ending its run September 16, 1921.

In 1922, Alfred S. Alschuler designed a seven-story addition to the building, at which time the theatre closed. Renamed the Blum Building, select women's clothiers featuring high-end fashions were on the ground floor. In the 1970s, the Torco Company purchased the building and added a large sign to the top of the building, which dominated the skyline. Columbia College acquired the building in 1990.

1909 Casino Garden Theatre/ 1911 Casino Theatre

By 1910 this was the fourth five-cent theatre within the Madison Street block, which was dubbed "Picture Row" (McQuade, *Film Index*, 20 August 1910). The Casino Garden at 58 West Madison Street, on the north side of the street, was typical: although only 25 feet wide, the theatre was 110 feet in depth. Typical of early theatres, the cashier's booth sat in the center of the entrance with entrance and exit doors to the right and left. The entrance also displayed the framed posters of the films exhibited and photographs of vaudeville actors. At night, the entrance was lit with nearly four hundred incandescent lights. The colored flashing sign displaying a clown juggling bits of fire was designed to draw people into the theatre.

The entire house, including the scenery used for vaudeville acts, was fireproof. A gardenlike effect was achieved in the lobby with a fence and ornamental lampposts. The seating capacity was 396 with a single aisle and the floor set at a pitch.

When the theatre opened, vaudeville was given preference with pictures used as chasers. A year later three good vaudeville acts and two reels of pictures were only presented on Saturdays and Sundays when the price of admission was raised to ten cents from a nickel on weekdays. Under the management of Harry B. Fitzpatrick, the Casino Garden was open from nine in the morning to eleven at night with continuous shows every day of about forty minutes in length. Each show presented a first-run reel with illustrated songs that were accompanied by two piano players and two singers. First-run films were changed every day (Morris, "Example of Modern Theater Construction"). In 1911, the theatre's name was shortened to Casino with Thomas Breskin as manager. The Casino Theatre closed in 1937.

Theatres Opening from 1910

The early silent movie theatres attracted Chicagoans downtown. At the same time the number of playhouses downtown prospered, and Chicago's Rialto (theatre district) flourished as a theatrical center second to none. Over time the nickel theatres became outdated. Larger, better-equipped photoplay houses were built with the development of feature films. Existing legitimate theatres were turned into moving picture theatres.

1910 Blackstone Theatre

Messrs. Charles Frohman, Klaw and Erlanger would combine to give Chicago "a theatre palace." The result was the Blackstone Theatre, designed by Marshall and Fox, at what is now 60 East Balbo Drive (Hubbard Court and Wabash Avenue). The theatre opened on December 31, 1910, with the premiere of the George Ade comedy, *U.S. Minister Bedloe*. Harry J. Powers, well known to theatregoers in the city, was manager for the first two decades (Percy Hammond, "Blackstone Opens, Beauty Praised").

The 1,400-seat interior was described as restful and refreshing with its ivory and green coloring. Two boxes were elevated as in the Princess Theatre. The most unique feature was the style of chair: a Pullman lounge, full-arm pattern that was intended to suggest clubhouse furnishings. This was a novelty in American playhouses but was found in various London theatres. The comfort of the chairs with their luxurious width was noted in the review of the opening performance. The lobby was finished in French walnut and gold.

Touring companies from New York were often on stage giving Chicagoans the opportunity to see actors such as Kathryn Hepburn, Vivien Leigh, Hume Cronyn and Jessica Tandy.

The first moving pictures shown at the Blackstone occurred on December 1, 1918.

Top: The facade of the Blackstone is a reproduction of the east wing of the palace at Versailles. *Bottom:* Elevators from the main foyer of Carrara marble took patrons to the balcony and gallery.

The Blackstone was purchased in 1988 by DePaul University for their Theatre School productions.

The Birth of a Race made its premier at the theatre, playing for a month. Two dollars was the price of admission; seats were sold out in advance of opening night. Joseph Breil, who composed the musical score for *The Birth of a Nation* also wrote the musical accompaniment for this film and personally conducted the orchestra on its opening night.

On March 6, 1933, the Blackstone closed with the play *The Bride Retires*. The house remained dark until the Federal Theater Project took it over in 1937. When the WPA theatre expired, the Blackstone went dark again from June 30, 1939, to February 19, 1940, when it opened with *Life with Father*, which ran for sixty-six weeks. In 1945 the Blackstone became part of the Shubert Organization joining the Harris, Selwyn, Great Northern, and Studebaker Theatres

(Claudia Cassidy, "On The Aisle," 17 October 1945). The last presentation at the Blackstone Theatre was Lily Tomlin's *The Search for Signs of Intelligent Life in the Universe.* When the theatre reopened in 1989, the stage floor was completely replaced, and state-of-the-art sound and lighting systems were in place. In 1992, it was renamed the Merle Reskin Theatre.

1911 Columbia Theatre/
1923 Adelphi Theatre/
1933 Clark Theatre

Built by the Chicago Gayety Company of New York City, the Columbia Theatre opened on February 27, 1911, with what was described as a mixture of farce, song and

The Clark Theatre from the corner of Clark and Madison streets.

dance called the *Ginger Girls*. The theatre occupied the ground floor of the new Planters Hotel Building at 7–19 North Clark Street, just north of Madison Street. There were three balconies and a seating capacity of 1,000 with plentiful exits. Built of fireproof construction, the theatre allowed its patrons to smoke but pumped 50,000 feet of fresh air a minute into the auditorium (Percy Hammond, "Concerning the New Columbia"). "Diluted burlesque" was the policy of the new theatre, part of the Columbia Burlesque circuit. A labor dispute against the circuit was waged in 1921 resulting in two bombs exploding in the Columbia Theatre ("Columbia and Star & Garter Are Attacked," *Chicago Daily Tribune*, 28 August 1921).

On December 30, 1922, A. H. Woods purchased the Planters Hotel Building including the Columbia Theatre property

making it Mr. Woods' third playhouse in Chicago. (He owned the Woods and Apollo theatres.) Mr. Woods opened his newly remodeled playhouse, renamed the Adelphi, on September 9, 1923, with the Lonsdale comedy *Spring Cleaning*. Critics applauded the intimate theatre richly decorated in gold and pale green with purple hangings (Butler, "Fine Cast in Bold Play at New Adelphi"). In 1924, Lionel Barrymore and Katherine Cornell appeared on stage. In the fall of 1932, when Chicago was faced with a shortage of amusements, the Adelphi presented a fantasy play called *The World Between* (Collins, "Chicago Gets Play of Home Grown Variety").

Remodeled into the Clark Theatre at 11 North Clark Street in 1933, it became one of the Loop's most unusual movie theatres. With seating reduced to 843, the Clark

The Clark Theatre in its last years.

showed more movies from the time it opened than any other theatre in Chicago.

Under the management of Bruce Trinz and his partner Howard Lubliner, the Clark introduced many unique policies. "Hark, Hark, the Clark" was a monthly program guide describing the coming attractions. The Clark Theatre initiated a policy of showing a different double feature every day, the only theatre of its kind in the country. These were movies ranging from the classic oldies to contemporary Westerns. The Clark's "Film Festivals" were special programs of outstanding films from Hollywood and Europe. The Sunday Film Guild was started in 1950 to rescreen two all-time film favorites each week. In 1955, the top films produced during the first twenty-five years of moviemaking were presented at a Clark Film Festival. Festivals in 1957 comprised Academy Award films with forty-seven Oscar winners. The theatre was open from dawn until dawn with low prices ($1.50 for adults and special discounts for students, servicemen, and seniors).

On June 26, 1970, the Clark Theatre discontinued its policy of two films per day and film festivals to become a first-run theatre. Movie critic Gene Siskel wrote, "With the death of the Clark's film festivals and retrospectives, Chicago loses one of its most important cultural assets, certainly our most important film institution" ("End of an Era," *Chicago Tribune*, 15 June 1970).

The Hawaiians was the first feature film under the Clark's new policy. The last double feature had been two behind-the-scenes films about Hollywood: *The Big Knife* and the original 1937 version of *A Star Is Born* with Janet Gaynor and Frederic March.

The showing of first-run films did not improve business, and owner Bruce Trinz felt he had no other option but to sell the theatre. In 1971, Kohlberg Theaters became the new owners. Until the Clark closed in 1974, adult films were featured. The entire block was eventually razed for the building of Three First National Plaza.

Kohl and Castle never went national and sold out to the Orpheum Circuit.

1912 Palace Music Hall/ 1926 Erlanger Theatre

The Palace Music Hall at 127–139 North Clark Street was in the City Hall Square Building next to the Grand Opera House. The Palace opened April 1, 1912, with a bill headed by the Leitzei sisters, the Tiller girls, and Thomas A. Wise, part of the Kohl and Castle vaudeville chain. The Music Hall was designed by C. A. Eckstrom with a seating capacity of 1,303. In addition to vaudeville, a Broadway musical was presented during the summer.

On December 1913, a variety show was presented at both the Palace Music Hall and the Majestic Theatre that included moving pictures of noted ballroom dancers Fred and Irene Castle dancing. On March 29, 1923, performances were halted to pay tribute to the memory of the great actress Sarah Bernhardt. All Orpheum Circuit theatres in the country observed the day of her funeral in Paris ("Bernhardt Honored Here," *Chicago Daily Tribune*, 29 March 1923).

A. L. Erlanger acquired the lease of the Palace Music Hall in January 1926 and renamed the theatre after himself. On October 10 of that year the newly remodeled Erlanger Theatre reopened with the four Marx Brothers in *The Cocoanuts*. The theatre now had a seating capacity of 1,500, which included the balcony. On January 16, 1927, Frederick Lonsdale's new play, *On Approval*, was the first play presented on stage without songs and dances.

From November to December 1927, while awaiting the arrival of Fred Stone to star in *Criss Cross*, the Erlanger Theatre presented *Wings*, the only silent film and first to win the Academy Award for Best Picture. The film starred Clara Bow and Gary Cooper in the story of World War I fighter pilots. Paramount's original picture release was color-tinted and would not be shown elsewhere in Chicago for one year (Tinee, "Wings Is Brilliant, Poignant, and in Spots Most Too Real"). The public had become infatuated with aviation after Charles Lindbergh's transatlantic flight. *Wings* was the first moving picture ever shown at the Erlanger.

Chicago's "most discussed" motion pic-

The "star" atop the theatre's entrance is just visible behind the light.

ture, Noel Coward's *Cavalcade*, was premiered at the Erlanger on February 8, 1933, on a reserved-seat basis. Also a Best Picture recipient, the Fox film presented the story of English life from New Year's Eve 1899 through New Year's Day 1933. The response prompted the movie's run to be extended.

On July 11, 1936, *The Great Ziegfeld* movie ended its run at the Erlanger. It had the longest engagement of any film offered in Chicago with performances at scheduled times on a reserved-seat basis. The MGM musical was the fictionalized biography of Florenz Ziegfeld whose father opened the Chicago Musical College in 1872. The three-hour epic starring William Powell, Myrna Loy, and Luise Rainer won Academy Awards for Best Picture, Best Actress, and Best Dance Direction. These three films appear to be the only movies shown at the Erlanger Theatre. It was during this time that Jones, Linick and Schaefer had been loosely affiliated with Mr. Erlanger's enterprises. (*Chicago Daily Tribune*, 26 July 1928.)

The Theatre Guild of the American Theater Society brought a series of comedies and Broadway hits to the Erlanger Theatre. Alfred Lunt, Lynn Fontanne, and Katherine Hepburn were some of the stars that appeared on stage. A revival of Gilbert and Sullivan operas was presented by the D'Oyly Carte Opera Company. Broadway musicals were also featured on its stage, especially in the 1950s.

The Erlanger's final curtain was on March 10, 1962, with *Bye Bye Birdie*. The Erlanger and remaining buildings on the block were razed to make way for the new Chicago Civic Center, now renamed the Richard J. Daley Center, Chicago's first major public building to be constructed in a modern rather than a classical architectural style.

1914 Star Theatre

The Star Theatre at 68 West Madison Street between Clark and Dearborn Streets was the fifth movie house to open in that block. The Pastime Theatre was next door.

In 1921, the Jones, Linick and Schaefer circuit purchased the 299-seat theatre. A year later they sold the theatre to the Harding Company, who converted the theatre into another of their Loop cafeterias. The theatre was then connected to the coffee shop at number 72.

1915 World Theatre

The World Theatre at 61 West Randolph Street, opposite the Garrick Theatre, opened on January 23, 1915. A pipe organ was installed in the theatre to accompany the action on screen. That same year smoke from a fire in the Nemo Shirt Company next door at number 65 emptied the theatre (*Chicago Daily Tribune*, 8 September 1915). Three years later the theatre closed.

1915 Rose Theatre

The Rose Theatre at 63 West Madison Street near Dearborn Street occupied the old Edelweiss Cafe site. The 299-seat theatre was the third built by Harry C. Moir. Before the Rose closed in 1929, the theatre featured the official Dempsey-Tunney fight pictures on January 24, 1927. On March 6, 1929, the only official Sharkey-Stribling fight pictures were presented by Jack Dempsey at the Rose Theatre (*Chicago Daily Tribune*).

1915 BandBox Theatre/
1923 Madison Theatre

The new $150,000 "Photoplay Palace" opened with Essanay's production of *In the Palace of the King* with "water-cooled and washed air" (*Chicago Daily Tribune*, 14 October 1915). The Band Box Theatre at 125–129 West Madison (between Clark and LaSalle streets) had a seating capacity of 299 and was managed by Jack Haag. Reviewing the theatre on January 6, 1916, the *Chicago Daily Tribune*'s movie critic called the new theatre "the most refreshing cinematic Loop spot." In 1923, it was renamed the Madison Theatre, only to close two years later. The theatre was demolished when construction began for First National Plaza.

1916 Castle Theatre

On the west side of the street at 6 South State Street, just south of Madison, the Castle Theatre opened in January 1916 as a movie house with a seating capacity of 297. The reviewers always referred to the Castle as the "little theatre" and found the picture "cottage" more comfortable and enjoyable than the larger picture palaces (Kelly, "Flickerings from Filmland," 2 May

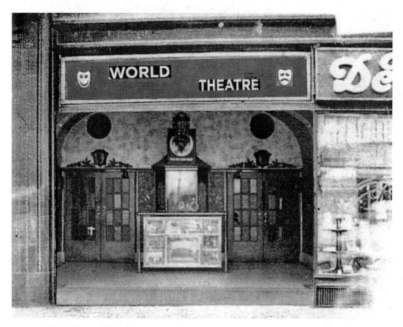

"The Loop's Newest Photoplay House" advertised Keystone comedies daily.

State Street entrance of the Randolph Theatre in 1925. Lillian Harvey was a very popular actress in Germany, and the features on the marquee were two early films.

1916). In 1929, the theatre was remodeled and wired for sound. In 1932, owner Clarence Beck converted the theatre into Chicago's first all-newsreel movie house. A thirty-minute show was presented for fifteen cents. Before long the Castle went back to presenting feature films with a newsreel and a serial (Tinee, "Castle Theater Goes Back to Feature Films"). Crowds would gather on the sidewalk to look at the poster display of what was

to be seen on screen and then would never come in to see the show! The western *Law and Order* was the first feature film with the change in policy. The Castle closed in 1935.

1918 Randolph Theatre

Designed by Henry L. Newhouse, the Randolph Theatre at 14–16 West Randolph Street was built for showing movies only, one of the earliest Loop movie houses without a stage. Jones, Linick and Schaefer opened the theatre on December 23, 1918, with Norma Talmadge in *The Heart of Wetona*, her just-released "western" feature, the only one she would make. Filmed during the Spanish influenza epidemic, her movie company was one of the few that did not shut down because the filming was done in a remote location. "The photography is so clear that you can almost smell the pine trees," wrote a movie critic (Tinee, "Right Off the Reel"). Performances were continuous from 8:30 A.M. to 11:00 P.M. Louis Jones assisted by Walter H. Moore managed the theatre. The entire front of the building was of cream and blue terra cotta, ornamented with rows of incandescent lights. The doorways were sheltered by Roman awnings. G. A. Brand hand painted scenes in the auditorium to represent an Italian garden and painted the ceiling sky blue. The 845 seats were upholstered in red leather. An organ was installed in the theatre.

To have two entrances (Randolph Street and State Street) was a rarity because of the added signage and staffing required at both box offices. A long hallway connected the two entrances.

On June 18, 1922, Universal Film Exchange leased the Randolph from Jones, Linick and Schaefer, beginning management on August 1. The theatre chain had decided that their new McVickers Theatre would feature moving pictures without vaudeville, putting them in direct competition with the Chicago, Roosevelt, and Randolph theatres. Movie fans would now be able to see every feature film at any one of four movie palaces in the Loop.

The Randolph Theatre closed on July 11, 1933, with a lecture and a presentation of the movie *Streets of Sorrow*. By 1934 it had been converted into the Old Heidelberg Restaurant, a Chicago landmark until it closed in 1963. Then Ronny's Steak House Restaurant (now in the James R. Thompson Center) made the building its home until 1999, after which the building was razed. A new building on the site incorporated the whimsical two-story Bavarian facade from the Old Heidelberg Restaurant. From 2002 to 2004, the building was home to the 153-seat Noble Fool Theatre (now Fox Valley Repertory). Today, it is the location of an Argo Tea Cafe.

1918 Woods Theatre

Originally built by Albert H. Woods as a legitimate theatre, the Woods Theatre on the northwest corner of Randolph and Dearborn streets, at 50 West Randolph Street, opened on March 11, 1918.

The play's first presentation, at the National Theatre in Washington, D.C., was applauded by President Woodrow Wilson: "Sentiments admirably represented in the play that I hope will soon sweep the world" ("Wilson Boosts Play That Will Open Theater," *Chicago Daily Tribune*, 6 March 1918). The play became a huge success.

The ten-story theatre and office building was designed by Marshall and Fox in a Neo-Gothic style. The building was on the site of the old Borden block designed by Dankmar Adler, the first building on isolated footings. There were two marquees on the building: one on the Randolph Street side, the other a terra cotta marquee on the Dearborn Street facade to complement the lighted niche on that side. Stores occupied the first floor of the corner building, while the upper floors were offices. On December 25, 1918, Lou M. Houseman left the management of the Woods Theatre and was replaced by J. J. Rosenthal.

The interior design was a mix of Middle Eastern and Indian styles. The curtain, chair covers, and carpets were in rich shades of purple and gold while the walls were paneled in walnut. All 1,200 seats had a full view of the stage.

In 1923, the Woods Theatre came under the management of Jones, Linick and Schaefer and featured first-run pictures.

The Woods Theatre Building was sold to the Essaness Theaters Corporation on August 6, 1938. The Woods Theatre was the first Essaness theatre in the Loop, and it became the flagship theatre for the circuit. Essaness promised a remodel and first-run movies. The lobby was altered from the original and doubled in width.

A barker could be seen in front of the Woods Theatre on September 12, 1938, announcing that two first-run pictures were being featured. *We're Going to Be Rich* marked the American screen debut of Gracie Fields, London cinema and music hall favorite. The second feature was *Bulldog Drummond in Africa*, which was an audience favorite. *Gone with the Wind* premiered on a reserved-seat basis in 1940 beginning an engagement that lasted the entire year. Danny Kaye's first movie, *Up in Arms*, played at the Woods for a year in 1944. In the 1950s, the marquee became unusually large. By the 1960s, the theatre had begun to deteriorate along with the choice of films playing on screen. In 1986 the Woods became part of the Cineplex Odeon theatre chain.

On Sunday, January 8, 1989, the Woods Theatre closed its doors with the films *Hellbound: Hellraiser II* and *I'm Gonna Git You Sucka*. The Woods was one of the last of the glittering movie palaces near the intersection of State and Randolph streets in the heart of the old Rialto. The Loop was without a movie theatre for the first time in nearly a century. The Woods Theatre was demolished the year it closed.

Top: The patriotic drama *Friendly Enemies* opened the Woods Theatre. *Bottom:* An early playbill for the Woods Theatre.

1908 Theatorium

A storefront photoplay house, the Theatorium at 178 North State Street was owned by V. C. Seaver. When it opened, the 299-seat theatre was the farthest north of the State Street nickelodeons. Admission was five cents to see the popular Charlie Chaplin movies featured at the theatre. The comedian at the time was part of Essanay Studios in Chicago on Argyle Street.

1919 State-Lake Theatre

Originally built as a vaudeville house for the Orpheum Circuit on land owned by the Marshall Field estate, the State-Lake Theatre at 190 North State Street opened on March 17, 1919, the largest house of the circuit. The opening program consisted of nine acts of standard vaudeville and two photoplays along with an organ recital.

G. Albert Lansburgh was the architect of the 2,649-seat theatre that occupied five stories of the office building. Sam Myers was the resident

1935 marked a change in the marquees on both sides. The Harris and Selwyn theatres can be seen behind the Woods on Dearborn Street.

manager. During its first six years of operation, the theatre was the biggest theatrical moneymaker in the city. "In the first three months the patronage was so heavy that all the carpets had to be renewed" ("Twenty Years Ago on State Street Rialto," *Chicago Daily Tribune*, 10 September 1933).

The walls of the auditorium were in old ivory and taupe. Eight loge boxes were on either side of the stage on the main floor and the balcony. Brocaded silk tapestries were used in the paneling and main curtain. All the draperies were of a red silk velour with appliqués of gold and turquoise blue satin. Seven aisles were on the lower floor of the auditorium. The elliptical dome suspended from the ceiling gave the effect of a sky because of its blue color and many tiny stars. A playroom and nursery were to be found on the third foyer of the balcony. The largest steel and asbestos curtain ever built for a local theatre was in place for the proscenium opening fifty-six feet wide and twenty-eight feet high.

When the State-Lake became the major venue for RKO Theatres in 1930 the theatre's vertical sign placed high on the building could be seen by Chicagoans for miles.

The theatre was acquired by Balaban and Katz on November 6, 1936, but their

Opposite top: This "karate thriller" was featured in 1976 and was representative of the films playing on downtown screens in the 1970s. *Opposite bottom:* Action films with Chuck Norris were popular in 1983.

management did not begin until May 1, 1937, as Jones, Linick and Schaefer had the lease until that date. Ben F. Lindheimer continued to manage the theatre through the transition, which was open from eleven in the morning to eleven at night. From 1935 through 1941, the State-Lake was one of the film houses (also the Palace, Chicago, and Rialto theatres) that presented stage shows or vaudeville acts along with feature films. In June 1940 Louis Armstrong appeared on stage.

The Robe, the first film in Twentieth Century–Fox studio's widescreen process called CinemaScope, opened at the State-Lake on September 23, 1953. This was the first CinemaScope screen in the Loop. *White Christmas* with Bing Crosby in VistaVision was presented on December 18, 1954. During the 1960s many first-run movies had their premiers at the State-Lake with long, successful runs, including the exclusive run of *Mary Poppins*.

On June 28, 1984, *Indiana Jones and the Temple of Doom* was the last film shown at the State-Lake. The theatre had been part of Plitt Theatres for a decade with Clayton Johnson as manager. "Only the Chicago Theatre was left on State Street," wrote Gene Siskel ("State-Lake Curtain Falls on June 28").

In 1986–1987, the interior of the State-Lake Theatre was gutted and remodeled by ABC Inc. into studios and offices for WLS-TV (Channel 7 in Chicago). The terra cotta facade of

Top: The State-Lake Theatre would be built on the site of the Theatorium. *Bottom:* The twelve-story State-Lake Building was designed by C. W. Rapp and George L. Rapp in a French Renaissance style similar to the Chicago Theatre across the street.

Top: The lobby was of polychrome terra cotta and marble. The marble stairs on either side led to three balcony foyers. *Bottom:* View of the auditorium from stage.

Left: View of the left side wall from main floor. *Right:* RKO's *Thirteen Women* in 1932 was not successful but today is considered a cult classic. *Bottom:* The State-Lake had the largest proscenium opening of any theatre in Chicago.

Left: The State-Lake Theatre held the Midwest premier of *Star Trek* in 1979. *Right:* The auditorium with a wide screen covering the proscenium opening.

the theatre was restored; the large marquee and ticket booth were removed. The auditorium was converted into two levels of broad-casting studios, including one that would accommodate a television audience of about 250 people.

Theatres Opening from 1920

During the twenties, Chicagoans went to see the new moving pictures, and when the talkies were introduced, even the Depression didn't keep them from seeing a show. This was the era of the grand movie palaces.

1920 Barbee's Loop Theatre/ 1923 Monroe Theatre

"Old Inter-Ocean Building to Be Made Theater" reported the *Chicago Daily Tribune* on May 20, 1918. The Ascher Brothers were reported to be converting the building into an over 3,000-seat movie theatre. This did not happen. The Inter Ocean building, designed by W. Carbys Zimmerman in 1900, housed the *Inter Ocean*, a Chicago daily morning newspaper so named as a symbol of Chicago's emerging global prominence. Before that, the Columbia Theatre stood on the site but was destroyed by a fire in 1900. However, in 1919, architects David Postle and John Fischer prepared plans to convert the building into a movie theatre ("Inter Ocean Building Will Be Movie House," *Chicago Daily Tribune*, 8 January 1919). The white matt-glazed architectural terra cotta front, restored with a thorough washing, was retained unaltered. The facade had not been cleaned in twenty years.

By the 1970s, patronage was down due to competition from the other Loop theatres showing adult fare.

The Monroe's marquee lit up in the 1930s.

The new theatre at 57 West Monroe Street, called Barbee's Loop after owner and showman William S. Barbee, opened on April 10, 1920, with the photodrama *She Loves and Lies* with Norma Talmadge, complete with symphony orchestra. The theatre could seat 1,120. In 1922, Mr. Barbee was blocked from installing a stage for vaudeville acts because of an insufficient number of emergency exits. Eventually the theatre closed (in May 1923) because of poor attendance.

Renamed the Monroe, the theatre reopened on Saturday, September 1, 1923, with the photodrama *The Silent Command*. The theatre became the Loop house for Fox films and would go on to showcase, in 1928, the new Fox Movietone process. Fox never built another Loop movie theatre. During the 1940s the theatre added the latest newsreels of the war to the program of feature films.

Giving the public what they wanted, James Jovan, owner and operator from 1957, played mostly B horror films until the mid–1960s. On Tuesday, January 20, 1959, the Monroe Theatre presented the Chicago premiere of the science fiction thriller *Plan 9 from Outer Space* along with *Time Lock*. The theatre's double-feature program was changed weekly playing from 9:00 A.M. to midnight. Eventually the theatre began an "adults only" policy showing soft-core porn.

A once crowded and clean theatre had deteriorated to the point of becoming rat infested. In January of 1975, the Monroe was one of six theatres shut down for "fire code violations" ("Six Loop Theaters Shut," *Chicago Tribune*, 23 January 1975). The ar-

The United Artists was in the heart of the Loop's theatrical district.

ticle noted that the other theatres — the State-Lake, McVicker's, Michael Todd, Cinestage, and Today — were also playing X-rated, violent movies. The theatre closed in 1977 and was demolished soon thereafter.

1921 Apollo Theatre/
1927 United Artists Theatre

The new Apollo Theatre at 45 West Randolph Street, on the southeast corner of Randolph and Dearborn, was built by A. H. Woods for the presentation of musicals. His Woods Theatre was on the opposite corner. This had been the site of the original Rice Theatre, recognized as the first theatre to be built in Chicago in 1847. The Howard Brothers in *The Passing Show* inaugurated the Apollo Theatre on May 29, 1921.

Holabird and Roche designed the three-story building in a Greek Revival style. The rounded entryway featured four two-story Corinthian columns. The auditorium resembled a classical Greek temple with a proscenium arch supported by Ionic columns. A frieze depicting a Greek procession decorated three walls. Light was provided by hanging bowls resembling Pompeian lamps. The seating capacity was 1,696 including the balcony.

On May 1, 1924, Messrs. Shubert took

Opposite page: The auditorium's blending of designs featured large, pierced inverted fan vaults supporting a somewhat pierced dome. The sidewalls contained four large murals by Steven Star representing a Moorish procession. All the pierced work was accented by concealed coves with lights that highlighted the gold leaf surfaces.

Top: United Artists Theatre in 1934. *Bottom:* 1940 advertising display.

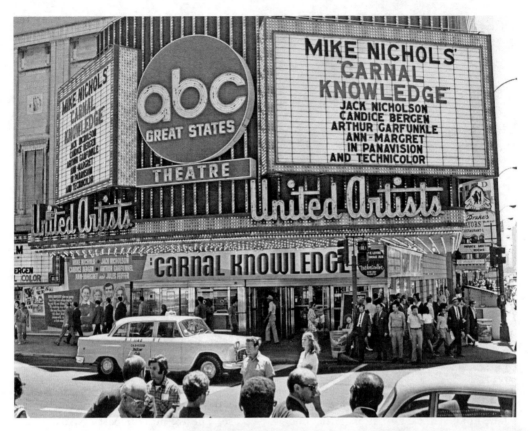

Top: A very different looking United Artists in 1971. *Bottom:* The lobby of the United Artists in 1978.

over management of the Apollo, operating and booking the theatre with an arrangement that gave part of the profits to Mr. Woods. Mr. Woods sold the theatre to the United Artists Corporation, a motion picture production and distribution company. The last show at the Apollo, *A Night in Paris*, was on February 18, 1927.

The United Artists Theatres Corporation (founded by D. W. Griffith together with Charlie Chaplin, Mary Pickford, and Douglas Fairbanks) took over the lease and completely gutted the building. The playhouse was completely turned around. A shallow stage was now at the Dearborn Street side with a lobby in place of the original stage, giving the theatre an imposing entrance on Randolph. An enormous vertical sign towered over the building on the Randolph Street side.

In 1928, within a radius of two blocks there were more than half of the legitimate

A large painting of President Theodore Roosevelt hung in the auditorium.

theatres of the city and many larger down-town motion picture houses, including the Chicago, Roosevelt, McVickers, and Oriental theatres. The interior of the theatre was redesigned for a film audience by C. Howard Crane in an eclectic mix of Spanish, Moorish, and Middle Eastern styles. A small vestibule and box office opened into a long, narrow lobby space. The black marble columns plus a carpeting pattern based on one from the Ottoman Palace in Turkey gave the lobby a Middle Eastern feel.

The United Artists Theatre opened with Norma Talmadge and Noah Beery in *The Dove* on December 26, 1927, becoming the debut venue in Chicago for all major United Artists releases. The increased seats now numbered 1,704. This would be a moving picture theatre without vaudeville. The theatre announced the presentation of D. W. Griffith's first sound picture, *The Battle of the Sexes*. The United Artists was said to be the most completely equipped theatre in Chicago for "Talking and Sound" installations (*Chicago Tribune*, 12 October 1928).

Balaban and Katz acquired the United Artists on April 2, 1929, the fifth movie palace they managed in the Loop and the fifteenth in Chicago. Business declined during the early years of the Depression prompting the United Artists to close for a few weeks during the summer of 1932.

The original towering vertical sign was taken down in the 1960s. In 1968 the United Artists Theatre became part of ABC-Great States, and Plitt Theatres from 1974 to 1985. Cineplex Odeon operated the theatre from 1986. Both Plitt Theatres and Cineplex Odeon were aware that condemnation proceedings could be brought against the building and invested as little money as possible into the theatre.

This once grand picture palace closed November 19, 1987, in a state of disrepair with a row of video games and a candy counter in its narrow lobby. The theatre building was demolished in 1989–1990 along with most of the adjacent properties in what came to be called Block 37. The city planned to redevelop the one-block parcel of land as part of its North Loop Redevelopment Plan. The Roosevelt Theatre, also in Block 37, had been demolished earlier.

1921 Roosevelt

"The Ascher Brothers to build a film house directly opposite Marshall Field &

Lobby of the Roosevelt Theatre.

Co.," reported the *Chicago Daily Tribune* on October 5, 1919. Architects C. Howard Crane and Kenneth Franzheim designed the theatre specifically to show movies, the twenty-eighth theatre built by the firm. At 110 North State Street, the theatre had a frontage on State Street of ninety feet. The Roosevelt Theatre opened on April 23, 1921, with the feature photoplay *Lessons of Love* starring Constance Talmadge. In addition to the feature movie, the Roosevelt Symphony Orchestra, a quartet of singers, and a ballet from *Aida* were presented.

President Harding, who had been invited to attend, congratulated the owners "on the dedication of this beautiful structure as a memorial to President Roosevelt. No name in our country's annals deserves better to be commemorated in the hearts and works of the people" ("Roosevelt Theater to Be Opened Today," *Chicago Daily Tribune*, 23 April 1921).

The Roosevelt was considered the Loop's finest movie house until the Chicago Theatre was built later that same year. The theatre was designed in a Greek Revival style with a facade of six faux columns below an ornately sculpted pediment.

A Kimball theatre organ had been installed in the theatre. The Roosevelt had a seating capacity of 1,535, but live stage shows were not presented.

The Roosevelt was acquired by Balaban and Katz with their management beginning on June 12, 1922, marking the end of an Ascher Brothers theatre downtown (Chase, "Smash Records with Roosevelt Theatre Lease"). This was Balaban and Katz's fifth house, and A. J. Balaban personally operated the theatre. The remodeled Roosevelt reopened with D. W. Griffith's *Orphans of the Storm* starring Dorothy and Lillian Gish.

The displays used on the front of the theatre were changed each week to advertise the new show, and over the years these tended to get larger. On June 26, 1936, the Joe Louis-Max Schmeling fight pictures were booked by Balaban and Katz as an extra screen attraction. On December 12, 1944, Balaban and Katz sold the Roosevelt Theatre to a New York syndicate.

The Loop was no longer the center of

Views of the proscenium from the main floor and balcony.

Top: Paramount Pictures released its silent epic the *Ten Commandments* in 1923. The Exodus scenes were photographed in early Technicolor. *Bottom:* In 1926 the marquee remained unchanged.

Top: The 1931 marquee included the Publix name. *Bottom:* Balaban and Katz advertising banners covered much of the facade in 1935.

entertainment it had been, and attendance at theatres had dwindled. The last show at the Roosevelt was on August 26, 1979, a double feature of *The Master Killer* and *The Chinatown Kid.* When its doors closed on Sep-

tember 1, 1979, the Roosevelt had been part of Plitt Theatres for four years. Ken Blewett had been manager since 1968. Chicago Tribune movie critic Gene Siskel reminded readers in his column of the "six theatres in the

Top: This 1954 marquee remained until the Roosevelt closed. *Bottom:* New Loop redevelopment plans forced the razing of the Roosevelt in 1979–1980.

Loop that had closed or had been demolished: Bismarck Palace, Michael Todd, Monroe, Clark, Loop, and Today (Siskel, "Roosevelt Theater Will Close Sept. 1").

1921 Chicago Theatre

Perhaps the most magnificent theatre of all, the Chicago Theatre at 175 North State Street was designed by C. W. Rapp and George L. Rapp for Balaban and Katz. The opening presentation on October 26, 1921, included Norma Talmadge in *The Sign on the Door* along with a fifty-piece orchestra; a

two-reel comedy, *The Playhouse*, starring Buster Keaton; and a concert on the theatre's Wurlitzer by Jesse Crawford (the Wurlitzer is now city-landmark protected). A white-gloved staff of over 125 ushers welcomed guests. Carl Sandburg reported on the opening for the *Chicago Daily Tribune* (Bernstein, *The Movies Are*). So great was the crowd that mounted police were required to keep order. Balaban and Katz called their Chicago Theatre the "Wonder Theatre of the World." The theatre came to be called the first "motion picture palace" in the nation.

A year after the Chicago opened, Balaban and Katz began their "Syncopation Week" which was so successful that jazz bands were a feature of the theatre's programming from the 1920s through the 1930s. Among the greats were Duke Ellington and Benny Goodman. John Phillip Sousa also brought his band to the Chicago stage.

The facade is covered in off-white terra cotta. The arch is sixty feet wide and six stories high, topped with an elaborate cornice. The window within the arch contains a circular Tiffany stained-glass panel with the coat of arms of the Balaban and Katz chain: two horses holding ribbons of 35-mm film in

Top: The Chicago Theatre's Mighty Wurlitzer. *Bottom:* People were standing eight abreast, at one time stretched completely around the block, to see the new theatre. The original marquee was simple without the theatre's name.

Top left: The State Street facade featured a replica based on the Arc de Triomphe in Paris. *Top right:* Grand lobby in 1921 from the entrance of the Chicago Theatre. *Bottom left:* 1921 view of the mezzanine just under the great window. *Bottom right:* Detail under balcony and mezzanine.

their mouths. Not long after the first marquee was put up, it was replaced by a new marquee with the now-famous design that features the "Y" insignia from Chicago's coat of arms. The "Y" represents the three branches of the Chicago River.

The vertical sign and marquee have served as an unofficial emblem of the city of Chicago. The vertical sign is original and one of the few in existence today.

From State Street, the theatregoer passes into an outer lobby through a second set of

Above: 1921 view looking toward the entrance inside the Grand Lobby. *Opposite top:* The "Y" is more prominent at night behind the horizontal word "Chicago" on the State Street side of the marquee. *Opposite bottom:* A picture of the early candy counter in the lobby, which was to be replaced in the 1953 remodel.

Top: The stairs rise and return on themselves from the lower level to the middle balcony level, a total of four full floors and one half floor. *Bottom:* View of the auditorium from the stage.

In the center of the proscenium arch is a large mural dating from 1932 of Apollo in his chariot, drawn by four white horses pulling the sun across the sky.

bronze doors into the Grand Lobby. The theatre was of grand proportions, the ultimate in opulence with gold leaf and crystal chandeliers inspired by the splendor of the Palace of Versailles in France ("New Chicago Film Palace Opening Draws Great Throngs," *Billboard*, 5 November 1921).

The majestic staircase in the five-story Grand Lobby was fashioned after that of the Paris Opera. The chandeliers would later be removed. The staircase ascends to the various levels of the Grand Balcony and is surrounded by gallery promenades at the mezzanine and balcony levels.

Top: The State Street entrance in 1935 prominently displaying the advertisements for their air-conditioned theatre. *Bottom:* Danny Kaye appeared on stage to celebrate the theatre's Twenty-fifth Silver Anniversary program.

Top: View of the large balcony and balcony boxes. The dome rises 110 feet. *Bottom:* The Chicago Theatre in 2010. (Photograph by the author.)

The Chicago Theatre's third marquee in 1948. Channel letters were again used, but were much larger in scale.

The auditorium at the main floor level is shaped like a horseshoe and has the unusual feature of being much wider than it is deep. Rapp and Rapp designed the backstage wall against an adjoining building to the east instead of to the north wall. The north wall of the building is a double brick wall with a sound barrier in between to shield the auditorium from the noise of the elevated train running above Lake Street.

Left: The post-war marquee featured extremely high side panels. *Right top:* The projection booth of the Chicago Theatre in 1955 with Brenkert Model BX80 projectors, RCA Model 9050 soundheads, and Motiograph magnetic penthouses mounted on top of the picture heads. (Courtesy John Watson.) *Right bottom:* The lobby during the 1953 remodel. Scaffolding covers much of the advertisement for the first 3-D movie.

At the balcony level the horseshoe shape of the main floor is reversed. Along the rear wall above the main floor is the shallow mezzanine, which seats about 400 people. Above the mezzanine and extending toward the proscenium over two-thirds of the main floor is the 1,500-seat balcony. The total seating capacity was 3,880 on opening, second in size only to the Auditorium. The balcony is supported by cantilevers to achieve unobstructed main floor sightlines, thereby eliminating the need for columns.

By 1926, the marquee was more elaborate with garlands of colored lights, large milk-glass attraction boards, and "Chicago" in large, illuminated letters on all three sides. Originally, the Chicago Theatre required 20,000 lightbulbs inside and out. "As they turned into State Street the Chicago sign blazed at them. Boy, was that a sign! It made daylight of the whole block" (Levin, *The Old Bunch*).

The theatre was completely redecorated in preparation for the 1933 Chicago World's Fair to accommodate the crowds of people that were expected. The original colors of wine, blue, and gold were considered too dark, and a new lighter color scheme was

The marquee in 1963 after being altered during the 1953 remodel. The front panel's display space was increased and the old-style track letters were retired.

used in shades of sienna with gold and silver highlights. The carpeting, draperies, and upholstery were replaced along with eight massive chandeliers in place of sidewall lighting coves. This was the first restoration ("Tivoli and Chicago Theatres Eightieth Anniversary Tribute," *Marquee*, 2001).

Movie attendance records remained at their peak during the 1930s and 1940s. People came to the Loop to visit a movie palace.

The displays used on the front of the theatre were changed every week with each new show, and over the years these tended to grow larger.

Twenty years after the first remodel, another remodel took place in 1953 when stage shows were discontinued. In an attempt to "modernize" the Chicago Theatre, many of the original furnishings and ornate light fixtures were removed. Simpler lines were in fashion. A false ceiling was added over the inner foyer, which closed the barrel-vaulted ceiling from view. The box office was rebuilt in bronze and stainless steel. There were new bronze entrance doors (Tinee, "Refurbishing of 'Flagship' Is Completed").

The Chicago Theatre premiered the first 3-D movie, *Bwana Devil*, on January 23, 1953. The movie starred Robert Stack and was based on a true story that occurred during the building of the first railroad in Central Africa. The Chicago Theatre drew the best in film entertainment from the year the theatre opened. The lobby was used as a "coming attraction" billboard. On May 1, 1953, the Chicago presented Warner Bros.' *House of Wax*, the first 3-D horror film, starring Vincent Price as the owner of a macabre wax museum. Having previewed some of the new film developments and techniques in Hollywood, the president of Balaban and Katz continued to feel that the new three-dimensional films with a new directional sound system would generate great public interest and be profitable for a large theatre like the Chicago (Tinee, "Theater Man Reports on the New 3-D Films").

With the introduction of CinemaScope, magnetic penthouses were used to "pick up" the four magnetic tracks on the film for stereophonic sound. The spare projector in the booth was common for the downtown movie palaces. However, in the Spring of 1965, two 35/70mm Century Model JJ projectors were installed for the Chicago premier of *In Harm's Way*, an American epic war film. It was the last black-and-white epic film made and the last black-and-white film starring John Wayne.

In 1968, Balaban and Katz became ABC-Great States Inc., and in 1974 Plitt Theatres was formed when it purchased the theatres of ABC-Great States. Downtown Chicago was beginning to change. Social and economic factors caused business to decline. As work started on State Street to transform it into a mall, newspaper critics wondered about the future of the theatre (Christiansen,

"A Grand Old Movie Palace Finds Itself on Shaky Ground"). The Chicago Theatre building was added to the National Register of Historic Places on June 6, 1979, and listed as a Chicago landmark on January 28, 1983. When Plitt Theatres closed the Chicago Theatre on September 19, 1985, three theatres remained open in the Loop: the United Artists, Woods, and Cinestage theatres (Siskel, "Chicago Theater to Close September 19 for Renovation").

Then in 1986 the Chicago Theatre was purchased by Chicago Theatre Restoration Associates, and assisted by the City of Chicago, a nine-month restoration of the theatre began, headed by Chicago-based architects Daniel P. Coffey and Associates and design consultants A.T. Heinsbergen and Company. Stained-glass windows were uncovered, as were the original elaborate ceiling decorations. The painted murals, plasterwork, and historic lighting fixtures were restored, the gilt was repainted, and the seats were renovated making the seating capacity 3,600. During this restoration, the height of the side panels was decreased, now looking more like the second marquee.

The Chicago Theatre reopened on September 10, 1986, as a performing arts venue starring Frank Sinatra on stage. He had performed at the theatre in the 1950s. The performers that followed included Bill Cosby, Liza Minnelli, Dionne Warwick, and Johnny Mathis (Christiansen, "Chicago Theatre Books Comeback").

Theatre Dreams Chicago, LLC, purchased the Chicago Theatre in 2003 from the City of Chicago and built a new basement-level theatre to present the comedy *Shear Madness*. MSG (Madison Square Garden) Entertainment, the live entertainment arm of Cablevision Systems Corporation, took over operation of the Chicago Theatre in 2008, their first facility outside New York City. MSG Entertainment said the Chicago Theatre would be programmed with popular and family entertainment, concerts, seasonal shows, and other live events (Jones,

"Chicago Theatre to Be Sold to Major New York Producer").

1922 Selwyn Theatre/1957 Cinestage Theatre/1985 Dearborn II

The Selwyn at 186 North Dearborn Street was designed as a legitimate theatre for stage productions built by and named for the celebrated New York producers, the Selwyn Brothers. A production of Somerset Maugham's comedy *The Circle* opened the theatre on September 18, 1922.

The walls of the auditorium were paneled with English walnut to contrast with the rich colors of antique green, cream, and gold used in the draperies and on the ceiling. The original seating capacity was 1,058 with Walter Duggan as manager.

1922 Harris Theatre /1958 Michael Todd Theatre/ 1985 Dearborn I

The Harris Theatre at 170 North Dearborn Street opened on October 2, 1922, with the comedy *Six Cylinder Love*. The theatre was named for Sam H. Harris, another New York theatrical producer who was an early partner of A. H. Woods and later George M. Cohan. The Harris was managed by Col. William Roche.

The interior design of the

Top, bottom and opposite page: The interior of the Selwyn took its inspiration from the English Renaissance.

Harris was inspired by the Italian Renaissance and originally sat 1,200 including the balcony. In contrast to the Selwyn Theatre, the walls of the Harris Theatre were paneled with Italian walnut embellished with intarsia (a mosaic worked in wood) and gold ornament. The curtains and draperies were of crimson velvet.

C. Howard Crane and Kenneth Franzheim were the architects of the Selwyn and Harris, always referred to as the twin theatres. They were designed exclusively as legitimate theatres and not as office buildings in which the theatres were incorporated. The limestone facades are ornamented with light-toned terra cotta. Round Roman arches frame statues of various mythological figures on the upper portion of the facade.

The development of sound films and the Depression caused a decline in attendance at live theatres. In the mid–1950s Michael Todd purchased the Selwyn and Harris theatres. The last theatrical production presented at the Selwyn Theatre was *A Hatful of Rain* in October 1956. The Harris

Theatre remained a legitimate theatre until 1958. The Selwyn was converted for wide-screen motion picture productions. The stage house, which was located at the rear of the theatre, was removed for a flat roof. The box seats and the entire stage were removed. The Selwyn reopened severely altered on April 4, 1957, renamed the Cinestage Theatre, with a curved strip screen and a standard curtain that opened horizontally. This was the first permanent Todd-AO showplace in Chicago. Michael Todd's *Around the World in 80 Days* had a long run.

Acquired by Plitt Theatres in 1974, the Cinestage began to advertise itself as "Chicago's Leading Adult Theatre" (*Chicago Tribune*, 4 January 1975). Shortly thereafter the Cinestage was one of six Loop theatres shut down for city violations. It was one of the largest crackdowns on movie theatres; all of the theatres (Michael Todd, State-Lake, McVickers, Monroe, and Today theatres) were showing X-rated or violent films ("Six Loop Theatres Shut," *Chicago Tribune*, 23 January 1975).

Top: The auditorium of the Harris Theatre. *Bottom:* The exterior design of both the Harris and Selwyn theatres complemented each other.

Top: The twin theatres were converted into movie theatres in the late fifties as the Cinestage and Michael Todd theatres. *Bottom:* The twin theatres before they were closed for good.

Michael Todd remodeled the Harris and renamed it the Michael Todd. The theatre reopened on December 26, 1958, with *Two for the Seesaw* (Claudia Cassidy, "Chicago Gets a Theatre for Christmas"). A false ceiling was installed, and the proscenium arch was removed as it was in the Selwyn. The theatre now had a large balcony and flat screen with a great waterfall curtain. Both theatres became showcases for reserved-seat

35/70mm Norelco Model DP70 projectors were installed in 1959. Norelco projectors were also in the booths of the Cinestage, McVickers and State-Lake theatres. (Courtesy John Watson.)

movie extravaganzas such as the *Sound of Music* and *Gigi*.

The Michael Todd was part of Trans-Beacon Theatres in 1968 when *Doctor Dolittle* was featured on a reserved-seat basis. ABC-Great States reopened and refurbished the Michael Todd on August 15, 1970. In 1974 the theatre became part of the Plitt theatre chain and was closed on April 22, 1977, for an indefinite period of time because of

poor attendance (Siskel, "Show's Over for Todd Theatre").

M&R Amusement Company leased both the Michael Todd and Cinestage theatres in 1985. Refurbished, the theatres reopened as first-run movie houses on Christmas Day 1985, renamed the Dearborn I and II. M&R had negotiated a reduced parking fee with a nearby garage to entice people to come downtown to see a movie (Siskel, "Todd, Cinestage Theaters Getting New Lease on Life"). However, the films on the screen soon became second-rate with adult themes. Both theatres eventually closed in 1988.

The Chicago Plan Commission added the Selwyn and Harris theatres to the list of buildings the city would save in the "North Loop renewal area" (Ziemba, "Two Theaters Regain 'Must-Save' Status"). In 1983, the twin theatres became a Chicago landmark. The theatres' landmark facades were saved and added to the list of Chicago landmarks in 1983. They would be incorporated into the new Goodman Theatre constructed on the site.

1926 Oriental Theatre

Crowds overflowed the Oriental Theatre at 24 West Randolph Street, opening on May 8, 1926, with Harry Langdon's comedy *Tramp, Tramp, Tramp* produced by First National Pictures. Paul Ash and his "Merry Mad Musical Gang" performed a three-scene syncopation production called *Insultin' the Sultan*.

Designed by C. W. Rapp and George L. Rapp for Balaban and Katz, the Oriental was their only Far Eastern–designed movie palace, one that would "charm away workaday worries and make it easy for audiences to forget

The Oriental Theatre occupied the ground floor of the twenty-two-story New Masonic Temple Building.

everything but the entertainment before them" ("Opening of Big Loop House Only Week Away," *Chicago Evening American*, 1 May 1926). Rapp and Rapp wanted to capture the spirit of the Far East in their design.

On the site of the famous Iroquois and Colonial theatres, the exotic Oriental Theatre presented first-run films and lavish stage shows with stars like Judy Garland, Al Jolson, and Sophie Tucker. Live jazz shows with Duke Ellington and his band were popular. The theatre earned a reputation as one of the city's best places to enjoy live performances.

A new feature in theatre construction was introduced in the revolving stage allowing one act to be in progress while two others were in preparation behind the scenes. The stage could be moved up, down, or sideways by motor power. The Oriental Theatre advertised this as its "magic flying stage" ("Oriental Theatre," *Theatre Historical Society of America*, 1997).

Black and gold marble was used in abundance along with pink Tennessee marble. Turbaned attendants added to the general atmosphere of the theatre meant to evoke memories of Indian bazaars. Wall lights consisted of elephant heads with tusks capped with golden balls, and massive foyer tables were supported by facsimiles of Indian elephants. The 3,238-seat auditorium evoked the jeweled splendor of the Far East with silks and velvets, ornate chandeliers, gold leaf, and terrazzo floors made with marble chips. The massive domed ceiling was rimmed with larger-than-life seahorses and goddesses. Painted columns and colorful plasterwork added to the look of an exotic Asian temple, as did the elephant-throne chairs that sat in an inner foyer. The scene on the curtain, painted on velour using metallic pigments imported from Japan, depicts "a conquering Indian rajah returning from victorious battle." ("Hails New Oriental as Wonder Theater," *Chicago Daily News*, 8 May 1926).

Rajahs from all over India come to-

Top: One of the Oriental's first marquees in 1927. The night shot shows the stud lighting surrounding the window. *Bottom:* The vestibule shows one of the Oriental's two inside box offices with an ornate cast-iron ceiling inset with glass panels.

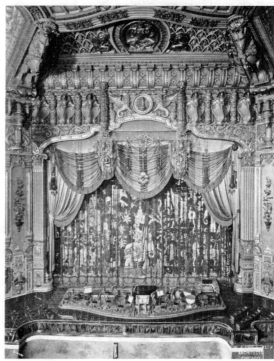

Left: The entrance hall was the tallest public space in the theatre rising through four levels. *Right:* The main curtain was made and decorated in Balaban and Katz's own scenery shop.

gether at the Durbar, an East Indian carnival and celebration in India, to display their wealth. The Durbar became an inspiration for the theatre. The Wurlitzer had also been ornately decorated when it was installed in the Oriental.

On January 31, 1946, Doubleday Company announced their purchase of the Masonic Temple building property, including the Oriental Theatre. Essaness Theaters Corporation then operated the Oriental and inaugurated a policy of showing the latest Hollywood movies. The only other Essaness theatre in the Loop was the Woods, which would fall under the same policy. The picture to inaugurate this new policy at the Oriental Theatre was *Breakfast in Hollywood* (1946), which was based on the 1940s morning radio program of the same name. The world premier of the Technicolor musical *I Wonder Who's Kissing Her Now* took place on June 29, 1947. The movie followed the career of Joe Howard, famous songwriter of the early

twentieth century. A parade on State Street included the stars of the movie: June Haver and Mark Stevens.

Like the other Loop theatres that remained open in the 1970s, the Oriental struggled to survive. M&R Amusement Company, owners from 1967, presented live performances in 1971 by such artists as Stevie Wonder and Gladys Knight in the hopes of drawing people to the theatre. That did not happen. Triple-feature kung fu movies were advertised in the mid–1970s.

The Oriental Theatre and office building were sold on November 18, 1978, and then leased and operated by Kohlberg Theatres. Also in 1978, in an effort to preserve the theatre, the Oriental was added to the National Register of Historic Places ("Oriental Theater Is Sold," *Chicago Tribune*, 18 November 1978).

The Oriental closed on January 4, 1981, the second largest movie palace in the Loop. The theatre had become a hangout for rival

gangs (Siskel, "Famed Oriental Theater Will Close as Film House").

For a time, a cordoned portion of the lobby was a business called Oriental Electronics. In 1996, Chicago mayor Richard M. Daley announced that the Oriental would be restored to its original grandeur. Daniel P. Coffey was the architect for the restoration (Christiansen, "Stage Set for Glittering Comeback by Oriental"). Plans included widening the theatre lobby and reducing the number of plush seats to 2,253 on three levels. The stage was deepened to sixty feet. A new marquee and a 110-foot vertical sign similar to the original was built for the Randolph Street entrance. The red, green, and gold marquee came with neon and blinking lights ("The Amazing Return of the Oriental," *Chicago Tribune*, 12 January 1996).

The renovated theatre reopened Octo-

Auditorium views with left side wall detail showing elaborate plaster ornaments.

ber 18, 1998, rededicated as the Ford Center for the Performing Arts Oriental Theatre with the Chicago premiere of *Ragtime* (Newman, "A Former Flapper Roars to Life, The Oriental Returns to Its 1920s Glory").

At present, it is the only movie palace known to have a Simplex XL projector with a Xenon arc lamp in their projection booth. (The Chicago and Palace theatres have no equipment in their booths.) The theatre is owned by the Nederlander Organization and operated by Broadway in Chicago. To bring the Oriental back to life was a harbinger of the revival of Randolph Street's theatre district.

1926 Palace Theatre

The "New Palace" Theatre was opened by the Orpheum Circuit as their flagship theatre with presentations of the highest class of vaudeville. The theatre had over 2,500 plush seats, all reserved for the two performances daily. Originally named the "New Palace" because there were ten other theatres in Chicago named "Palace" at the time of opening, the theatre was part of the Eitel block, consisting of the twenty-two-story Metropolitan office building and the New Bismarck Hotel. Commissioned by Emil and Karl Eitel, the building filled the entire block from LaSalle to Wells streets, with the theatre entrance at 151 West Randolph Street. The Eitel brothers had purchased the old Germania Hotel in 1894, which

Crowds overflow the auditorium in 1969 at the final concert on the Oriental's Wurlitzer.

The second marquee, here in 1956, is topped by one of the White Way electric signs, which character-
ized theatres in the Loop.

The Ford Center for the Performing Arts in 2010 (photograph by the author).

stood at Randolph and LaSalle streets, and had it razed to build the new building.

The inaugural performance was Monday evening, October 4, 1926. The Orpheum Circuit had placed an advertisement in the *Chicago Daily Tribune* (23 September 1926) to announce their move from the Palace Music Hall to Chicago's most distinctive new playhouse. The New Palace Orchestra was lead by Dan J. Russo. A dedicatory address was given by Mayor William E. Dever followed by nine acts of Orpheum Circuit vaudeville for their new flagship theatre. Emil Eitel was president of the hotel and theatre on opening.

The interior of the Palace evoked the atmosphere of the palaces at Fontainebleau and Versailles from the Grand Lobby with its breche violet and white marble through a succession of lobbies and foyers with Italian marble walls, crystal chandeliers, gold plaster ornamentation, and massive decorative mirrors. The mezzanine is unique in that it consists entirely of loges, one adjoining the other without partitions. Elevators carry patrons to the mezzanine and balcony levels.

Bob Hope, Sophie Tucker, and Mae West were some of the stars that played the Palace. In the late 1920s and early 1930s, audiences began to lose interest in vaudeville, prompting the conversion of the Palace in 1930 into a movie house.

At the end of May and the beginning of June 1930, RKO (Radio-Keith-Orpheum) initiated celebrity vaudeville with "big talking pictures" at popular prices. There were continuous performances starting at 11:00 A.M. The RKO Palace set records in attendance ("Big RKO Shows Lead Loop," *Chicago Daily Tribune*, 7 June 1930).

Legendary architects C. W. Rapp and George L. Rapp designed the entire block.

Ethel Barrymore appeared in a one-act comedy at the Palace, her first Chicago engagement in a "cinema-vaudeville house" ("Miss Ethel Barrymore to Be at Palace," *Chicago Daily Tribune*, 4 August 1933). In August 1934 ballroom dancers Veloz and Yolanda appeared on the stage of the Palace, as did Ann Southern in October 1936, adding song to her program of dance.

Otto K. Eitel (Karl's son) and James Coston, manager, announced the coming of Cinerama to the Palace Theatre on July 30, 1953. This was a new wide-screen, multiple-projector film presentation. The entire mezzanine of the Palace was taken over for three co-ordinated projection booths suspended from the balcony floor. Three separate films were projected simultaneously by three projectors. This provided a left-hand, center, and right-hand view of the subjects, giving an impression of depth and reality. The 26 × 27 foot screen curved across the entire front of the theatre from wall to wall. The first Cinerama film was *This Is Cinerama* narrated by Lowell Thomas with a thrilling roller-coaster scene that had everyone talking. All seats were reserved for every performance. The cost ranged from as low as $1.25 during the week to as high as $3.60 for Saturday night. The film ran for ninety-nine weeks to June 13, 1955. "The Only Cinerama Theatre within 300 Miles" headlined the *Chicago Tribune* (July 16, 1955) when *Cinerama Holiday* played. The last Cinerama film, *South Seas Adventure* ended at the Palace on No-

The Grand Lobby of the Palace Theatre.

Top left: The main staircase of the Palace Theatre. *Top right:* View of a left side box. *Bottom left:* The ceiling dome is visible from the balcony. *Bottom right:* RKO was now managing the theatre offering vaudeville entertainment to supplement the program of movies.

Top: Foyer of the Palace Theatre. *Bottom:* Mezzanine promenades flank the grand foyer on all sides.

The arrangement of seats is such that even the last row in the auditorium is close to the large stage.

made since Cinerama was first introduced, this presentation required only a single booth (Tinee, "This Is Cinerama Returns").

Cinerama helped the Palace retain its reputation as a premier theatre. After the Cinerama equipment was moved to the McVickers Theatre, the Palace became known as the Bismarck Theatre in 1965. The Bismarck installed two 35/70mm Norelco Model DP70 projectors. The theatre was the scene of the Midwest premier, on January 27, 1966, of *Dr. Zhivago*, complete with red carpet, klieg lights, and a quartet of Russian-costumed balalaika musicians strolling in the theatre lobby. Seats were sold on a reserved-seat basis. James Michener's story of *Hawaii* premiered in October of 1966.

From 1976 to 1984, the management of the Bismarck Hotel transformed the auditorium of the theatre into the Pavilion Room of the hotel by removing the seats on the orchestra level and bringing the floor flush with the stage. An entrance door was created from the hotel lobby into the mezzanine level of the theatre. Another connection was made from the main floor of the theatre

vember 1, 1959. Manager Douglas Helgeson reported that another record had been set: Cinerama pictures had run for six years.

This Is Cinerama was rereleased and returned to the Palace on June 28, 1961, with four shows daily at popular prices. Because of the technical improvements that had been

Top: View of the right side of the auditorium from main floor. *Bottom:* The Cadillac Palace in 2010. (Photograph by the author.)

Left: The renamed Cadillac Palace in 1999. *Right:* The doormen with new uniforms in 1946.

to a service area of the hotel to facilitate the movement of food from the hotel's kitchen to the auditorium. The Pavilion Room served as Chicago Democratic Party headquarters and was used by many civic organizations.

Early in 1984, the theatre was converted into a rock venue, but later that year a portion of the elevated floor collapsed under the weight of dancing fans, bringing an end to the venue.

By the end of 1999, the Palace was completely restored to its original Versailles-like elegance. Samples of the original fabric used in the theatre including the original Aubusson carpets, draperies and trims had been archived and accessed. Seating on the orchestra level was reconfigured for better sightlines. Three aisles were eliminated to create a large center seating section. The 2,300-seat Palace included orchestra, dress circle and balcony. The expanded stage, 110 feet wide and 45 feet deep, could now support any

show. The Cadillac division of General Motors purchased naming rights, and a new eight-foot vertical marquee was installed.

Broadway in Chicago reopened the Cadillac Palace on November 12, 1999, with Elton John and Tim Rice's *Aida*, the Tony Award-winning Best Musical. Another bright light had returned to the revived Randolph Street theatre district.

1929 Civic Opera House and Civic Theatre

The Civic Opera House opened on November 4, 1929, in a building with a forty-five-story office tower and two twenty-two-story wings at 20 North Wacker Drive. (The Civic Opera Building became a Chicago landmark in 1998.) A group of Chicago businessmen led by Samuel Insull wanted Chicago to have its own opera house.

Designed by Graham, Anderson, Probst,

Top: The architects commissioned Henry Hering to produce architectural sculpture for the building. *Bottom:* The entrance of the Civic Opera House. The Civic Theatre was at the north end of the block-long building.

View of the auditorium from the large stage.

and White in a French Renaissance Revival style in the shape of a large throne, the building faces the Chicago River between Washington and Madison streets. A colonnaded portico runs the entire length of the building on the Wacker Drive side. The opera house interior features gilt cornices, Austrian crystal, travertine marble, and an imposing double staircase. A seating capacity of 3,563 includes the main floor, mezzanine boxes, and two balconies, making it the second largest opera auditorium in North America.

In 1954, the Civic Opera House became the permanent home of Chicago's world-renowned Lyric Opera Company. Manager J. Charles Gilbert announced that on June 20, 1958, the Opera House would depart from its usual fare and present the Midwest premier of *Windjammer* in Cinemiracle. All seats were by reservation. Adventure on the high seas, romantic ports of call, and breathtaking scenery were some of the highlights to be seen on "the biggest movie screen in the world" ("Adventure at Sea, Scenery Ingredients of Cinemiracle," *Chicago Tribune*, 25 May 1958). The Cinemiracle cameras covered a span of 146 degrees horizontally and 55 degrees vertically with a field of vision approximating that of the human eye. The film had a new seven-track stereophonic high fidelity system, vivid color photography, and a musical score by Morton Gould. The Cinemiracle motion picture process utilized three 35-mm cameras, but rather than projecting the image on a strictly straight photographic principle, Cinemiracle made additional use of angled mirrors to create an all-encompassing picture ("Cinemiracle — It's Done with Mirrors," *Chicago Tribune*, 8 June 1958). The production closed September 27, 1958, to make way for the start of the Lyric Opera season.

Another group of businessmen led by Harley Clarke wanted Chicago to have a theatre devoted to Shakespeare. The Civic Theatre opened November 11, 1929, with a production of *Hamlet*. On October 1, 1933, Chicago was introduced to a gala radio premier over WBBM of a new revue with Olsen and Johnson, comedy stars of the legitimate stage.

The Civic Theatre was the site of successful plays, including the premier of Tennessee Williams' *The Glass Menagerie*. It was the first midwestern theatre to offer the 1944 English motion picture *Henry V*, which played for twenty-six weeks. Laurence Olivier starred in the recreation of the stage production of Shakespeare's play performed at the Globe Theatre. On September 17, 1948, the Civic Theatre was reconstructed with 878 seats for its conversion to a television studio for station WENR-TV, the city's third video outlet ("Civic Theater Will Become Video Studio," *Chicago Daily Tribune*, 29 August 1948). The Civic Theatre closed in 2003 to be torn down so that improvements could be made to the stage and set areas of the Civic Opera House.

Top: Interior of the Telenews Theatre. *Bottom:* Crowds in front of the Loop Theatre lining State Street to welcome home astronauts from the Apollo 11 space flight.

1939 Telenews Theatre/ 1953 Loop Theatre

The theatre, housed in its new building at 165 North State Street, opened December 23, 1939, featuring newsreels, cartoons, and other short subjects in a one-hour program. The theatre was designed by Shaw, Naess, and Murphy for Midwest Newsreel Theatres Inc. of Chicago. This theatre of 606 seats was technically next door to the Chicago Theatre but separated by a wide alley called Benton Place. The small lobby of the Tele-

news Theatre featured an operating United Press Teletype. The Telenews was simple in decoration with a balcony to handle the main-floor overflow.

The newsreel was born in October 1896, when Thomas A. Edison invented a popcorn popper and realized he needed a way for people to learn of it. Edison's next attempt to film news as it was made occurred a year later when he filmed the Corbett-Fitzsimmons fight in Carson City, Nevada. The films of President Taft's inaugural ceremonies in 1909 inspired the Pathe brothers, French motion

Top: The Telenews was the first news theatre built in downtown Chicago. *Bottom:* Detail of the marquee.

picture producers, to open the first newsreel theatre in Paris ("Tower Ticker," *Chicago Daily Tribune,* 18 October 1949).

The Telenews Theatre changed its name to the Loop Theatre and began a new policy of presenting first-run pictures on April 8, 1950. The theatre opened with the *Red Shoes* at popular prices. On July 16, 1950, the Loop returned to its original name and policy, once more becoming the Telenews Theatre, showing one-hour programs of newsreels, topical events and short subjects.

The Metropolitan Opera's *Carmen* was presented from the stage in New York City through closed-circuit network television on December 11, 1952. This was a successful fundraiser for the Metropolitan Opera Company with Fritz Reiner conducting the orchestra. All seats for the Chicago showing were six dollars. After this showing, the Telenews became the Chicago outlet for what was described as the first national sales conference ever executed by closed-circuit theatre television.

On December 25, 1952, "a sea lion jumped off the screen and into the audience at the Telenews, but nobody got hurt or even splashed" (*Chicago Tribune*). The occasion was the premier of the Tri-Opticon stereo movie system developed in London and brought to this country by Sol Lesser. Two pictures were shown on the screen, one for

Gene Siskel Film Center in 2010. (Photograph by the author.)

the right eye and one for the left. They corresponded to the views our eyes would see in the original setting. Patrons had to wear Polaroid glasses to ensure that each eye saw only the correct view.

In 1953, the theatre became the Loop again, part of the Brotman and Sherman theatre chain. The theatre became known as "The Little Giant of the Loop" and was highly profitable even though surrounded by large movie palaces (Siskel, *Chicago Tribune*, 21 May 1972).

The theatre housed an electronics store after it closed in 1978. In the same building, but around the corner at 8 East Randolph Street, a new "Loop Theatre" opened in August 2003 to provide interim performing space in the downtown area for legitimate theatre companies. However, in January 2005, the entire building was razed, including the (old) Loop, to make way for a new residential/retail development.

2000 Gene Siskel Film Center

The Film Center of the School of the Art Institute of Chicago (SAIC) was founded in 1972 to present premiers of new American and foreign films, revivals of classics, independent productions, and retrospectives. In 2000 the Film Center was renamed to honor the late *Chicago Tribune* film critic and Film Center supporter Gene Siskel.

Chicago's oldest and largest not-for-profit theatre became part of the revitalization of the Loop. (Photograph by the author.)

The Gene Siskel Film Center moved on June 1, 2001, to 164 North State Street, the most state-of-the-art movie facility in the Midwest. Across the street from the Chicago Theatre, the film center comprises a 264-seat auditorium and a 64-seat smaller theatre. Over one hundred programs are presented every month. A small cafe area allows patrons to meet before and after the show.

2000 Goodman Theatre Center

With a city committed to revitalizing its Loop and a major gift to ensure the use of the Goodman name, a new theatre was built on the site of the Harris and Selwyn theatres, utilizing their landmark facades ("The Goodman Picks a Perfect Spot," *Chicago Tribune*, 8 January 1992).

The new Goodman Theatre at 170 North Dearborn Street opened in December 2000 with August Wilson's play, *King Hedley II*. There are two modern auditoriums, named the Albert and the Owen, after two members of the Goodman family who continue to be major donors.

The Goodman Theatre was founded as a tribute to Chicago playwright Kenneth Sawyer Goodman, who died in the 1918 influenza epidemic. Goodman's parents donated monies to the Art Institute of Chicago to establish a professional repertory company and a school of drama at the Art Institute. The opening ceremony on October 20, 1925, featured three of Kenneth Sawyer Goodman's plays: *Back of the Yards*, *The Green Scarf*, and *The Game of Chess*. The theatre's first artistic director, Thomas Woods Stevens, built the new theatre's repertory with a mix of classics, contemporary hits, experimental, and new plays, a formula that the theatre generally follows to this day. In 1976 the Goodman separated itself from the Art Institute, incorporating as the Chicago Theatre Group Inc. Two years later the Goodman School of Drama was acquired by DePaul University.

South State Street Theatres

At different times called "Whiskey Row" and "Museum" or "Burlesque Row," cheap amusement places and saloons populated the outer fringes of Chicago's great retail street, especially south of Van Buren Street. Clusters of dime museums, penny parlors, arcades, dance halls, and burlesque theatres stood side by side with rooming houses, gambling dens, and "resorts."

Many theatres populated South State Street throughout its heyday. Some were open for a short time, some changed their name often, while others just faded away and left no record.

1881 Park Theatre

On September 10, 1881, the Park Theatre, at 333–335 State Street (old street number), opened. This was one of the historical playhouses that burned in the Great Fire, was rebuilt, and then was destroyed again in 1873. When the theatre was reopened, the new Park Theatre was soon referred to as a "disreputable resort" running indecent performances. A bar adjoined the main entrance of the theatre ("The East Side of State Street," *Chicago Daily Tribune*, 30 March 1883). King, Suits & Company owned the theatre until March 30, 1896, when Tri-State Amusement Company purchased both the Park and the next-door Hopkins' Theatre. Col. Hopkins would absorb the Park to enlarge his playhouse ("Events of a City Day," *Chicago Daily Tribune*, 25 March 1896).

1884 People's Theatre/1895 Hopkins' Theatre/1904 Folly Theatre/ 1919 State-Congress Theatre

In the early 1890s, the People's Theatre was host to plays, acrobatic and specialty performers, and boxing matches. At 531 South State Street, the People's had experienced hard times and was closed for several months in 1894. The theatre reopened on February 11, 1894, under the direction of Col. J. H. Haverly, presenting popular attractions at popular prices. A comedy, *The Circus Queen*, was presented ("Reopening of the People's Theatre," *Chicago Daily Tribune*, 11 February 1894).

In 1895, a St. Louis showman, Col. John Hopkins, leased the People's Theatre, naming it after himself. The Hopkins' opened on February 10, 1895, with a performance of Frederick Brayton's play *Forgiven*. An eight-act vaudeville program was also included. The theatre had a seating capacity of 1,477.

The "old" Park Theatre next door was used as the entrance to the Hopkins' Theatre. When Tri-State Amusement Company purchased both theatres, the Hopkins' Theatre was enlarged. The old Park was used to make room for the construction of a new larger entrance, lobby, and foyer. The front and intervening walls between the two theatres were demolished. The auditorium was extended back to the street wall providing accommodation for several hundred more people. On reopening, the local stock company presented *Pink Dominoes* with a vaudeville list made of entirely new attractions.

Col. Hopkins was credited with originating the "10–20–30" vaudeville show in Chicago, or "continuous vaudeville" ("Col. John Hopkins Showman Is Dead," *Chicago Daily Tribune*, 25 October 1909). On July 5, 1896, the Hopkins' Theatre showed moving pictures of New York's Herald Square, a boxing match, and *Picture of a Kiss*, reported to be the first confirmed commercial exhibition of movies in Chicago (www.southloophistory.org). Even standing room was difficult at the Hopkins' Theatre after Col. Hopkins introduced Edison's Vitascope. The views were changed every week in addition to the vaudeville program and a comedy drama.

With a change in policy to a combination of vaudeville and burlesque shows on August 21, 1904, the theatre, now renamed the Folly, was managed by John A. Fennessey. One block south was the Trocadero, and both theatres continued to find their way into the news with reports of immoral shows. The Folly Theatre inaugurated amateur night on Fridays in 1907 with the prize being five silver dollars. On July 1, 1908, headlines read, "Burlesque at the Trocadero and Folly to be eradicated in the interest of public morals. Productions have sunk into the ooze of filth" (*Chicago Daily Tribune*). On November 18, 1913, the Folly was closed by Deputy Commissioner Dougherty for alleged violations of building ordinances. The Folly was again mentioned (even though it was closed) as being next door to one of numerous phony medical businesses on South State Street ("Quacks Driven Out of Chicago," *Chicago Daily Tribune*, 24 April 1915).

Renamed the State-Congress, now with 1,020 seats, the theatre reopened on November 22, 1919, with Charles D. Peet as manager. The theatre offered a program of "high-grade continuous vaudeville" with eight big vaudeville acts and a feature picture for twenty-two cents. However, when attendance did not increase, the theatre reverted back to burlesque. A fire and explosion of incendiary origin following a union dispute caused South State Street police to close the State-Congress in 1933 (*Chicago Daily Tribune*, 29 October 1933). Earlier that year both the Rialto and State-Congress theatres advertised weekly changes to their burlesque and cinema programs. In 1935, the theatre building was demolished for a "motor parking place" (Collins, "Stage Landmark Becomes Park Place").

1897 Savoy Theatre/
1899 Trocadero Theatre

Mr. Clifford advertised his Gaiety Theatre on Washington Street along with the notice of his new "10–20–30" Savoy Theatre to open on October 3, 1897. A comedy, *The Gay Matinee Girl*, was the opening feature. Siegel, Cooper & Company, one of Chicago's largest dry goods establishments, was across the street. A year later, on Thanksgiving, a small riot broke out at the Savoy causing police to close the theatre. The trouble started when manager Frank Mott absconded taking the box office receipts with him ("Starts a Riot at the Savoy," *Chicago Daily Tribune*, 25 November 1898).

The City Club Burlesque Company then reopened the theatre at 414–416 South State Street on September 2, 1899, renamed the Trocadero. The manager, T. E. Miaco, remarked that this would be a straight burlesque house, free of "vulgar features" ("News of the Theaters," *Chicago Daily Tribune*, 2 September 1899). The "Troc," advertised as the "New Burlesque Palace," with 957 seats became a well-known and notorious burlesque house continuously pushing the boundaries of public decency. The four-story building fronted forty feet on State Street with a depth of one hundred feet. In 1904 John Fulton was manager of the theatre. ("Mayor Harrison Visits Levee District and Closes Variety Shows," *New York Times*, 30 September 1911). A new all-female burlesque troupe performed every week with shows continuing until the theatre closed (Chase, "Old Trocadero Theater Sold for $190,000").

Purchased by Stebbins Hardware Company, the building housed retail stores until being demolished in the mid–1970s. The Harold Washington Public Library, Chicago's main library, is on the site.

1907 Premier Theatre

Another Jones, Linick and Schaefer theatre, the Premier at 336 South State Street featured a program of vaudeville acts and moving pictures.

The July 29, 1911, issue of *The Moving Picture World* wrote that even though the Premier was a vaudeville house the projection was far superior to that of the average straight picture show in the Loop. The 299-seat theatre closed in 1915 to be razed for the larger Rialto Theatre to be built on the site by the "movie kings."

1909 U. S. Music Hall/1933 State-Harrison Theatre/ 1956 Gayety Theatre/1961 Rialto Theatre

The 288-seat U.S. Music Hall at 546 South State Street was managed by Sol Fitchenberg. On February 24, 1916, the *Chicago Daily Tribune* announced that the U.S. Music Hall, along with the Gem and Chicago theatres, would be closed three days "for the practice of lewdness." Those theatres were called "the filth of South State Street." The U.S. Music Hall reopened featuring a movie and burlesque.

The theatre was renamed the State-Harrison in 1933, initially a motion picture house that eventually reverted to burlesque. On December 31, 1954, Mayor Kennelly revoked the amusement license of the State-Harrison Theatre for presenting indecent performances.

Rialto Theatre in the 1970s.

The theatre reopened in 1956 called the Gayety until 1960. In 1961 it reopened renamed the Rialto Theatre and would become one of the last bastions of burlesque in Chicago. Mayor Daley closed down the theatre from November 1967 to August 1970, and again on February 5, 1972, for code violations.

Explosions rocked both the Follies and Rialto theatres in 1974. In the Rialto the explosions "occurred from behind the stage, blasting into the audience completely destroying the movie screen" ("Bombs Rock Three Porno Houses; Dynamite Sticks

Top: The Gem Theatre in 1910 with its facade from the Decorators Supply Company. *Bottom:* The Gem Theatre in 1941 before the marquee burned in October 1946. (Courtesy of Eric Bronsky Collection.)

Found in Fourth," *Chicago Tribune*, 15 November 1974). The bombings appeared to have been caused by stick bombs placed in the rear of the building. The Rialto closed briefly then reopened with "Triple Adult Programs" at bargain rates. The city closed the theatre for good late in 1975.

1909 Gem Theatre/
1950 Follies Theatre

In its early days, the Gem Theatre at 450 South State Street featured moving pictures along with vaudeville and comedy acts. Early in his career, comedian Red Skelton appeared on the theatre's stage. The 480-seat Gem eventually became known for its burlesque shows.

From 1916 the theatre was under constant scrutiny by the Political Equity League, headed by Mrs. Guy Blanchard. The League made recommendations to censors about the immoral nature of movie houses. Mrs. Blanchard had publicly made comments about the dancing girls at the theatre, complaining that they were "drug fiends," and that there were small rooms in the theatre where the girls could indulge their habit. One of the dancers "shot" back at Mrs. Blanchard, saying that the "girls who dance at the Gem theater work there and do the dances they do so they can make a living" ("Gem Theater Girl Dancer Answers Women Accuser," *Chicago Daily Tribune*, 2 February 1916). Manager Sidney H. Selig met with the group that had closed the theatre later that February. ("State Street Theaters Get Consent of Women Who Closed Them Up," *Chicago Daily Tribune*, 24 February 1916).

Chicago police raided the theatre on many occasions, and when the theatre became the Follies in 1952 striptease acts would eventually be used to attract patrons into the theatre. Those stage shows ended when the theatre was closed in 1972.

A bomb in November 1974 closed the Follies, but the fire that started in the lobby of the old theatre in 1978 destroyed the building (Sjostrom, "Follies, a Shady Lady of Theater, Dies in Fire"). Today, the Harold Washington Library Center is located on the site.

1917 Rialto Theatre/
1931 Loop-End Theatre/
1944 Downtown/
1950 Minsky's Rialto

The Rialto Theatre at 336 South State Street, near the corner of Van Buren Street, was built in 1916 for the Jones, Linick and Schaefer circuit. The theatre opened January 23, 1917, as a venue for both feature photoplays and vaudeville. The entertainments were continuous from 11:00 A.M. to

Top: Spelling out its name in lights and with a façade from the Decorators Supply Company, the Premier Theatre opened in 1907. *Bottom:* By 1974 the Follies had become an X-rated movie house.

The Rialto was five stories high with a facade of white terra cotta and granite.

11:00 P.M. Rothschild's Department Store (later Goldblatt's Department Store) was across the street.

Designed by Marshall and Fox with a mosaic-tiled vestibule, a lobby of marble, and slightly over 1,500 seats, the interior of the Rialto occupied a lot size of 98 by 100 feet with the auditorium placed diagonally within that square.

The organ and air supply occupied the

space usually reserved for the boxes. The walls were paneled with old rose and gold brocade. By 1919 the theatre had added burlesque. Gypsy Rose Lee and Fannie Brice were some of the performers that appeared on stage.

From 1931 to 1936 the theatre was renamed the Loop-End featuring photoplays and variety shows still owned by Jones, Linick and Schaefer. Mayor Kelly revoked the licenses of six establishments along South State Street's burlesque row, including the Rialto Theatre on October 27, 1937. Ten days earlier the police had raided the same establishments for indecent performances.

The night of August 24, 1944, marked the last performance of burlesque at the Rialto Theatre. "For a quarter of a century brassy-voiced hawkers peddled suggestive novelties during intermission. Burlesque was rapidly becoming extinct" ("The End of the

Top: Smoking was permitted in the smaller mezzanine balcony as a feature of the theatre. *Bottom:* The marquee of the Rialto in 1929 with an added horizontal sign.

Rialto Burlesque," *Life Magazine*, 18 September 1944).

After a complete redecoration, reconstruction and modernization, the theatre reopened on September 1, 1944, under new management renamed the Downtown Theatre, presenting stage attractions, motion pictures, and centering attention on name bands. The opening featured Johnny "Scat" Davis and his orchestra, with Duke Ellington and his orchestra booked for later in the month.

In late April 1950, Minsky, the biggest name in burlesque, took over the theatre to make the Rialto Chicago's leading burlesque house. Minsky played a key role in the careers of Phil Silvers, Red Buttons, and Abbott and Costello, taking them out of vaudeville and putting them in burlesque where he said "they learned valuable lessons in comedy." Minsky's Rialto announced a movie program with four stage shows daily. The theatre closed January 1, 1954, at the end of the New Year's Eve show, to the *Chicago Tribune's* headline "Girls Take-Em Off for Last Time at Rialto." The final sign on the marquee told the story: "Speedway Wrecking Company (The Greatest Stripper of Them All" (*Chicago Tribune*, 1 January 1954). Air-conditioned retail shops were to be built on the site.

SMALL SOUTH STREET THEATRES CLUSTERED ALONG SEVERAL BLOCKS SOUTH FROM VAN BUREN STREET

1906 Royal Theatre

This small theatre at 408 South State Street primarily showed movies. For a brief time from 1911 to 1916 it was called the Royal Turkish, but in its last year became the Royal again. The Harold Washington Library Center, Chicago's public library, is now on site.

1907 Unique Theatre

This 299-seat theatre at 350 South State Street was situated just north of the Premier Theatre and next door to the Wonderland Theatre. Part of the Jones, Linick and Schaefer circuit, the Unique was open for only three years.

1908 Wonderland

The Wonderland at 352 South State Street was a nickel theatre, part of the large Mills Edisonian Arcade. A large manufacturer of illustrated song machines, the Mills Edisonia Company owned and operated both the theatre and arcade. The Wonderland closed in 1912.

1908 American Theatre

The American at 522 South State Street featured four acts and pictures for five cents. Sidney Selig owned the 250-seat theatre, which was eventually closed down by Mayor William Hale Thompson in 1916. The Chicago Women's Church Federation, a moral reform organization, wanted burlesque eliminated within the city of Chicago and was constantly exerting pressure on the mayor to close the theatres down.

1909 National Theatre

A dime museum was combined with the 277-seat National Theatre at 608 South State Street. Four acts and pictures made up the bill. *Variety* reported that business was so good that the adjoining building would be acquired to increase the seating capacity to 900 ("State Street Theatres," 19 June 1909). The National was one of the theatres cited in 1911 as being a peril to the public because of a lack of adequate emergency fire exits ("Film Theaters Peril to Public"). The National closed in 1962.

1909 Chicago Theatre/
1933 Joyland Theatre

The Chicago Theatre at 614 South State Street was managed by the Hulquist Brothers. The theatre had 270 seats and was renamed the Joyland in 1933. The Joyland remained open until 1952.

1911 Paris Theatre/
1916 Fashion Theatre

The 242-seat Paris Theatre at 557 South State Street was between Congress Parkway and Harrison Street. The theatre closed in 1914 and reopened as the Fashion Theatre in 1916 managed by Charles Fidiles. The Fashion closed in 1952.

1914 Paris Theatre

Down the street at 618 South State Street was the "new" Paris with a seating capacity of 274, managed by Henry Bambara. This theatre remained open until 1958. Three years later, renamed the Gayety Paris, the theatre reopened only to close two years later.

Appendix A

Downtown Chicago
Theatre Circuits

Tri-State Amusement Company

In 1896, Tri-State Amusements joined with Col.
John Hopkins to form a vaudeville circuit. In
1897, Kohl and Castle, proprietors of the Olympic
Theatre and Chicago Opera House among others
formed a booking partnership with Col. Hopkins
and the Tri-State Amusement Company to feature
high-class vaudeville.

Park/Hopkins	1896–1898
Dearborn	1898–1903

Jones, Linick and Schaefer

The firm was one of the largest theatre chains in
Chicago in the early days of moving picture exhibition. They started by opening the first nickel
theatre in a storefront in the Palmer House block
on December 25, 1904 (Caward, "The Rise of
Jones, Linick & Schaefer").

Royal	1906–1911
Hale's Tours	1906–1906
Orpheum	1907–1925
Bijou Dream	1907–1922
Premier	1907–1915
Unique	1907–1910
Alcazar	1907–1929
Lyric	1907–1915
American	1908–1916
Comique	1908–1909
National	1909–1911
Gem	1909–1916
Boston	1912–1921
Colonial	1913–1924
LaSalle	1913–1927
McVickers	1913–1926; 1934–1961

Studebaker	1914–1917
Star	1914–1922
Rose	1915–1929
Lyric	1916–1921
Rialto	1917–1944
Randolph	1918–1922
Woods	1923–1938
Erlanger	1927–1936
State-Lake	1933–1937
Majestic	1934–1934

Alfred Hamburger Theatres

The Alfred Hamburger theatre circuit included the
Louise Amusement Company, with theatres in the
Hyde Park and Kenwood neighborhoods, and the
Alfred Theatre Company ("Hamburger Enterprises
Now in New Quarters," *Inter Ocean*, 18 May 1913).
During World War I, Alfred Hamburger was one
of the largest circuits in Chicago, with almost all of
the circuit's theatres in Chicago neighborhoods.

Fine Arts	1912–1916
Comedy	1914–1915
Ziegfeld	1914–1919

Orpheum Circuit Inc.

Martin Beck started the Orpheum Circuit in 1919
eventually merging with a chain of theatres owned
by B. F. Keith and Edward F. Albee to form Keith-
Albee-Orpheum ("Orpheum and Keith-Albee Are
Merged," *Chicago Daily Tribune*, 9 December
1927). Albee partnered with J. P. Kennedy's Hollywood film company to form Radio-Keith-
Orpheum (RKO) Studios. When Kennedy took
control the Orpheum Circuit became a chain of
movie houses.

State-Lake	1919–1930
Majestic	1921–1930
Palace	1926–1930

Ascher Brothers Theatres

The Ascher Brothers built a picture house directly opposite Marshall Field and Company on State Street. The Roosevelt Theatre opened in 1921, but just a year later the ever-expanding Balaban and Katz chain acquired the theatre. The Ascher Brothers chain of community theatres at that point consisted of twenty-six theatres in the Chicago area and Wisconsin.

Roosevelt	1921–1922

Balaban and Katz (becoming ABC-Great States Inc.)

Balaban and Katz became the most profitable movie theatre chain in the country. They would come to dominate cinema in Chicago from the twenties. Their innovations and philosophy caused other theatre owners to follow in their footsteps. Renowned stage shows with the latest feature films, service from a troupe of ushers, and air conditioning were trademarks of Balaban and Katz theatres.

In 1925 Balaban and Katz merged with Hollywood's largest studio, Famous Players- Lasky (Paramount Pictures), giving them access to Hollywood's top films. The Publix theatre chain was the result of the merger. Publix-Balaban and Katz merged with the American Broadcasting Company in 1953. On June 5, 1968, Balaban and Katz was renamed ABC-Great States Inc. to identify the company more closely with its parent organization. ABC-Great States reopened a refurbished the *Michael Todd Theatre* on August 15, 1970 (until 1974).

Chicago	1921–1974
Roosevelt	1922–1944
McVickers	1926–1934
Oriental	1926–1946
United Artists	1929–1968
Garrick	1934–1960
Apollo	1934–1949
State-Lake	1937–1974

Fox Theatres

William Fox was a pioneer in the movie theatre business and during the mid–1920s set out to acquire movie palaces. In the mid–1930s he merged with Twentieth Century Pictures to become Twentieth Century–Fox. The *Monroe Theatre* became the Loop house for Fox films and would go on to showcase, in 1928, the new Fox Movietone process.

Monroe	1923–1949

Lubliner and Trinz

On July 15, 1925, Balaban and Katz purchased seventeen Lubliner and Trinz movie theatres, none in downtown Chicago. The theatre circuit for a very short time managed Orchestra Hall. The Clark Theatre, under the ownership and management of Bruce Trinz and partner Howard Lubliner, introduced many unique policies.

Orchestra Hall	1924–1925
Clark	1933–1971

Warner Bros. Pictures

On June 29, 1925, Warner Bros. Pictures subleased the *Orpheum Theatre* from Jones, Linick and Schaefer to premier their movies. In 1927, "Vitaphone" appeared on the marquee announcing Warner's sound-on-disc system.

Orpheum	1925–1937

RKO Theatres Corporation (former Radio-Keith-Orpheum Corp.)

RKO was formed so that the Keith-Albee-Orpheum vaudeville theatres could be converted into movie houses ("Big RKO Shows Lead Loop," *Chicago Daily Tribune*, 7 June 1930). They went out of business in 1957 as a movie producer.

Palace	1930–1952
State-Lake	1930–1933
Woods	1930–1933
Grand	1942–1957

Essaness Theaters Corporation

Essaness Theaters acquired the *Woods Theatre* on June 18, 1938, from Jones, Linick and Schaefer, their first Loop theatre. On January 31, 1946, the Doubleday Company purchased the Masonic Temple Building property, which included the *Oriental Theatre*. Essaness Theaters then operated the Oriental, inaugurating a policy of showing the latest Hollywood movies.

Woods	1938–1986
Oriental	1946–1967

Brotman and Sherman Theaters Inc.

Brotman and Sherman became one of the Midwest's largest independent theatre circuits. Downtown, their Loop Theatre was one of the most profitable theatres from 1969 to 1971. Even though it was surrounded by movie palaces, the Loop earned the nickname "the Little Giant" (Siskel, *Chicago Tribune*, 21 May 1972). In 1981, Plitt Theatres purchased the theatres of Oscar Brotman and Leonard Sherman.

Loop	1953–1978

M&R (Marks and Rosenfield) Amusement Company

This family-operated theatre chain purchased the Oriental Theatre and Masonic Temple Building on August 28, 1967. In 1982, M&R began operating the Studebaker Theatre and World Playhouse as Fine Arts 1 and 2, eventually constructing two more theatres to become the Fine Arts Theatres. M&R leased both the Michael Todd and Cinestage theatres, renamed the Dearborn I and II after being refurbished.

Oriental	1967–1978
Fine Arts	1982–1989
Dearborn I and II	1985–1988

In 1989 M&R became part of Loew's Inc. The Fine Arts Theatres closed in 2000 owned by Loews Cineplex Entertainment.

Kohlberg Theaters

Stanford Kohlberg founded his theatre chain with the purchase of a drive-in theatre in Oak Lawn, Illinois. He retired in 1987 and sold his theatres and drive-ins.

Shangri-La	1970–1980
Clark	1971–1974
Oriental	1978–1981

Plitt Theaters Inc.

Plitt Theatres formed in 1974 when it purchased the movie theatres of ABC-Great States Inc., which included the Balaban and Katz theatre chain (Siskel, "Movie House Wars"). In August 1985, the Plitt movie theatre chain was purchased by Cineplex Odeon Corporation.

Chicago	1974–1985
Cinestage	1974–1985
State-Lake	1974–1984
Michael Todd	1974–1977
United Artists	1974–1985
Roosevelt	1975–1979

Cineplex Odeon Corporation

Cineplex was founded in 1979 and in 1984 purchased Canadian Odeon Theatres to become Cineplex Odeon. In 1998, Cineplex Odeon merged with Loews Theatres to form Loews Cineplex Entertainment Corporation. In 2006, AMC Theatres merged with Loews Cineplex Entertainment with the merged company adopting the AMC name ("AMC Closes Acquisition of Loews Cineplex," *USA Today* 26 January 2006).

United Artists	1986–1987
Woods	1986–1989

Appendix B

Downtown Chicago's Historic Movie Theatres

Theatre	Address	Open	Close	Seats
Adams	20 East Adams Street	1921	1933	650
Adelphi (see Clark)				
Alcazar	69 West Madison Street	1907	1929	300
American	522 South State Street	1908	1916	250
American Music Hall (see Eighth Street)				
Apollo	74 West Randolph Street	1928	1949	1,383
Olympic (1879–1927) (1,994 seats)				
Metropolitan (1878–1879)				
New Chicago (1875–1878) (984 seats)				
Kingsbury Hall (1873–1875)				
Apollo (see United Artists)				
Aryan Grotto (see Eighth Street)				
Astor	12 South Clark Street	1922	1949	300
Auditorium	50 East Congress Pkwy.	1889	open	3,877
Band Box (see Madison)				
Barbee's Loop (see Monroe)				
Bijou Dream	114 South State Street	1907	1922	296
Bismarck (see Cadillac Palace)				
Blackstone	60 East Balbo Drive	1910	1988	1,400
Boston	79 West Madison Street	1908	1912	300
Boston	21 North Clark Street	1912	1921	400
Brooke's Casino (see Eighth Street)				
Cadillac Palace	151 West Randolph Street	1999	open	2,300
Bismarck (1965–1975) (2,150 seats)				
RKO Palace (1930–1952)				
Palace (1926) (2,300 seats)				
Capri	66 East Van Buren Street	1958	1968	375
Ziegfeld (1952–1958)				
Studio (1940–1952)				
Sonotone (1935–1940)				
Punch & Judy (1930–1935) (375 seats)				
Central (1920–1929) (850 seats)				
Central Music Hall (1915–1919)				
Comedy (1914–1915)				
Howard's Comedy (1913–1914)				

Theatre	Address	Open	Close	Seats
Whitney's Opera House (1907–1913)				
New (1906–1907) (850 seats)				
Steinway Hall (1895–1906) (700 seats)				
Casino	58 West Madison Street	1911	1937	396
Casino Garden (1909–1911)				
Casino Garden (see Eighth Street)				
Castle	6 South State Street	1916	1935	297
Central (see Capri)				
Central Music Hall (see Capri)				
Chicago	175 North State Street	1921	open	3,600
Chicago (see Eighth Street)				
Chicago (see Joyland)				
Cinestage (see Dearborn II)				
Civic Opera House	20 North Wacker Drive	1929	open	3,563
Civic	20 North Wacker Drive	1929	2003	878
Clark	11 North Clark Street	1933	1974	920
Adelphi (1923–1933) (1,550 seats)				
Columbia (1911–1923)				
Cleveland's (see Strand)				
Cohan's Grand (see RKO Grand)				
Coliseum (see RKO Grand)				
Colonial	24 West Randolph Street	1905	1924	1,724
Hyde & Behman's (1904–1905)				
Iroquois (1903)				
Columbia (see Clark)				
Comedy (see Capri)				
Comique	204 South State Street	1908	1909	250
Cort	126 North Dearborn	1909	1934	962
Cozy/Kozy	40 South Clark Street	1915	1929	275
Crystal Palace (see Strand)				
Dearborn (see Garrick)				
Dearborn I	170 North Dearborn Street	1985	1988	1,058
Michael Todd (1958–1977)				
Harris (1922–1958)				
Dearborn II	186 North Dearborn Street	1985	1988	1,058
Cinestage (1957–1985)				
Selwyn (1922–1956)				
Downtown (see Rialto)				
Eighth Street	741 South Wabash Ave.	1924	1960	1,200
Aryan Grotto (1918–1924)				
Chicago (1915–1917)				
American Music Hall (1909–1915)				
Garden (1908–1909)				
Brooke's Casino (1905–1908)				
Casino Garden (1884–1905)				
Electric	101–103 South State Street	1904	1905	100
Erlanger	127–139 North Clark Street	1926	1962	1,500
Palace Music Hall (1912–1926)				
(1,303 seats)				
Fashion	557 South State Street	1916	1952	242
Paris (1911–1914)				
Fine Arts	410 South Michigan Avenue	1982	2000	+/- 1,500
World Playhouse (1933–1972)				
(500 seats)				
Playhouse (1916–1932) (546 seats)				
Fine Arts (1912–1916)				
Music Hall (1899–1912) (400 seats)				
Studebaker (1898–1978) (1,200 seats)				

Theatre	Address	Open	Close	Seats
Follies	450 South State Street	1950	1974	480
Gem (1909–1950)				
Folly	526 South State Street	1921	1937	300
Folly (see State-Congress)				
Ford Center for the Performing Arts	24 West Randolph Street	1998		2,253
Oriental (1926–1981) (3,238 seats)				
Four Cohans (see RKO Grand)				
Garden (see Eighth Street)				
Garrick	64 West Randolph Street	1903	1960	1,257
Dearborn (1898–1903)				
Schiller (1892–1898) (1,270 seats)				
Gayety (see Rialto)				
Gayety	618 South State Street	1961	1963	274
Paris (1914–1958)				
Gem (see Follies)				
Gene Siskel Film Center	164 North State Street	2000	open	328
Globe (see Strand)				
Grand Opera House (see RKO Grand)				
Great Northern	21 West Quincy Street	1896	1959	1,400
Hippodrome (1912–1920)				
Lyric (1910–1912)				
Hale's Tours of the World (see Orpheum)				
Hamlin's (see RKO Grand)				
Harris (see Dearborn I)				
Hippodrome (see Great Northern)				
Hopkins' (see State-Congress)				
Howard's Comedy (see Capri)				
Hyde & Behman's (see Colonial)				
Illinois	61–65 East Jackson Street	1900	1934	1,287
International (see Strand)				
Iroquois (see Colonial)				
Joyland	614 South State Street	1933	1952	270
Chicago (1909–1932)				
Kingsbury Hall (see Apollo)				
LaSalle	110 West Madison Street	1902	1949	900
Loop	165 North State Street	1953	1978	606
Telenews (1939–1953)				
Loop End (see Rialto)				
Lyric	320 South State Street	1916	1921	286
Lyric (see Great Northern)				
Lyric (see Strand)				
Madison	127 West Madison Street	1923	1925	299
Band Box (1915–1923)				
Majestic (see Shubert)				
McVickers	25 West Madison Street	1857	1984	2,264
Metropolitan (see Apollo)				
Michael Todd (see Dearborn I)				
Minsky's Rialto (see Rialto)				
Monroe	57 West Monroe Street	1923	1977	950
Barbee's Loop (1920–1923) (1,120 seats)				
Music Hall (see Fine Arts)				
National	608 South State Street	1909	1962	277
New (see Capri)				
New Chicago (see Apollo)				
Olympic (see Apollo)				
Omar	532 South State Street	1909	1916	299
Orchestra Hall	220 South Michigan Avenue	1904	open	2,581
Oriental (see Ford Center for the Performing Arts)				

Theatre	Address	Open	Close	Seats
Orpheum	110 South State Street	1907	1937	799
Hale's Tours of the World (1906)				
Automatic Vaudeville (1900–1905)				
Palace (see Cadillac Palace)				
Palace Music Hall (see Erlanger)				
Paris (see Fashion)				
Paris (see Gayety)				
Pastime	21 West Adams Street	1908	1914	250
Pastime (see Today)				
People's (see State-Congress)				
Playhouse (see Fine Arts)				
Premier	336 South State Street	1907	1915	299
Princess	319 South Clark Street	1908	1937	982
Punch & Judy (see Capri)				
Randolph	14 West Randolph Street	1918	1933	845
Rialto	336 South State Street	1917	1954	1,574
Minsky's Rialto (1950–1954)				
Downtown (1944–1950)				
Loop End (1931–1936)				
Rialto	546 South State Street	1961	1975	288
Gayety (1956–1960)				
State-Harrison (1933–1954)				
U.S. Music Hall (1909–1933)				
RKO Grand	119 North Clark Street	1942	1958	1,400
Four Cohans (1926–1928)				
Cohan's Grand Opera House				
(1912–1926)				
Grand Opera House (1880–1912,				
1928–1942)				
Hamlin's (1878–1880)				
Coliseum (1875–1878)				
RKO Palace (see Cadillac Palace)				
Roosevelt	110 North State Street	1921	1979	1,535
Rose	63 West Madison Street	1915	1929	299
Royal	408 South State Street	1906	1917	299
Royal Turkish (1911–1916)				
Royal Turkish (see Royal)				
Savoy (see Trocadero)				
Schiller (see Garrick)				
Selwyn (see Dearborn II)				
Shangri-La	222 North State Street	1970	1980	482
Shubert (Bank of America)	18 West Monroe Street	1945	open	2,016
Majestic (1906–1934)				
Sonotone (see Capri)				
Star	68 West Madison Street	1914	1922	299
State-Congress	531 South State Street	1919	1933	1,020
Folly (1904–1913)				
Hopkins' (1895–1904) (1,600 seats)				
People's (1884–1895) (1,477 seats)				
State-Harrison (see Rialto)				
State-Lake	190 North State Street	1919	1984	2,649
Steinway Hall (see Capri)				
Strand	348 South State Street	1915	1915	500
Lyric (1907–1915)				
Strand	700 South Wabash Ave.	1915	1921	975
Globe (1909–1914)				
International (1906–1909)				
Cleveland's (1903–1906)				

Theatre	Address	Open	Close	Seats
Crystal Palace (1890–1903)				
Studebaker (see Fine Arts)				
Studio (see Capri)				
Telenews (see Loop)				
Theatorium	178 North State Street	1908	1916	299
Today	66 West Madison Street	1941	1975	327
Pastime (1908–1939)				
Trocadero	414 South State Street	1899	1915	957
Savoy (1897–1899)				
Unique	350 South State Street	1907	1910	299
United Artists	45 West Randolph Street	1927	1987	1,704
Apollo (1921–1927)				
U.S. Music Hall (see Rialto)				
Whitney's Opera House (see Capri)				
Wonderland	352 South State Street	1908	1912	299
Woods	50 West Randolph Street	1918	1989	1,200
World	61 West Randolph Street	1915	1918	299
World Playhouse (see Fine Arts)				
Ziegfeld	624 South Michigan Ave.	1909	1922	738
Ziegfeld (see Capri)				

Bibliography

General References

Bronsky, Eric, and Neal Samors. *Downtown Chicago in Transition*. Chicago: Chicago's Books Press, 2007.

Chicago History Museum, The Newberry Library. http://encyclopedia.chicagohistory.org.

Gomery, Douglas. *Shared Pleasures: A History of Movie Presentation in the United States*. Madison: University of Wisconsin Press, 1992.

Hall, Ben M. *The Best Remaining Seats: The Golden Age of the Movie Palace*. New York: DaCapo Press, 1988.

Margolies, John, and Emily Gwathmey. *Ticket to Paradise: American Movie Theaters and How We Had Fun*. Boston: Little, Brown, 1991.

National Register of Historic Places. www.nationalregisterofhistoricplaces.com.

Naylor, David. *American Picture Palaces: The Architecture of Fantasy*. New York: Prentice Hall, 1981.

Naylor, David, and Joan Dillon. *American Theaters: Performance Halls of the Nineteenth Century*. New York: Wiley, 1997.

Putnam, Michael. *Silent Screens: The Decline and Transformation of the American Movie Theater*. Baltimore, MD: Johns Hopkins University Press, 2002.

Theatre Historical Society of America. www.historictheatres.org.

Valentine, Maggie. *The Show Starts on the Sidewalk: An Architectural History of the Movie Theater, Starring S. Charles Lee*. New Haven, CT: Yale University Press, 1994.

Williams, Michael, and Richard Cahan. *Richard Nickel's Chicago: Photographs of a Lost City*. Chicago: CityFiles Press, 2008.

PART I

Acland, Charles R. *Screen Traffic: Movies, Multiplexes, and Global Culture*. Durham, NC: Duke University Press, 2003.

Adams, Rosemary K., ed. *A Wild Kind of Boldness: The Chicago History Reader*. Grand Rapids, MI: Eerdmans, 1998.

"Amusements." *Chicago Daily Tribune*, 9 October 1872.

Balaban, David. *The Chicago Movie Palaces of Balaban and Katz*. Chicago: Arcadia Publishing, 2006.

Bommer, Lawrence. "Coming Up: The Loop at Night Downtown (But Not Out) in Chicago." *Chicago Tribune*, 14 November 1986.

Cassidy, Claudia. "Whatever Happened to Downtown?" *Chicago Tribune*, 12 August 1973.

Caward, Neil G. "The Rise of Jones, Linick & Schaefer." *Motography*, 26 December 1914.

"Censors Inspect Nickel Theatres; Find Many Bad Shows in Them and Worse in the Penny Arcades." *Chicago Daily Tribune*, 1 May 1907.

Chase, Al. "Balaban & Katz Acquire State Lake Building." *Chicago Daily Tribune*, 7 November 1936.

_____. "Balaban & Katz Sells Roosevelt Theater, Takes 25 Year Lease." *Chicago Daily Tribune*, 12 December 1944.

_____. "Movie War on Rialto Seen in Universal Move." *Chicago Daily Tribune*, 18 June 1922.

"Chicago-Midwest 1986 Conclave." *Marquee, Journal of the Theatre Historical Society of America* 18, no. 2 (1986).

"Chicago's Line-Up in Fall Promises Active Film Battle; Jones, Linick & Schaefer and Balaban & Katz Preparing — Have All Loop Houses — Expect Bigger Pictures." *Variety*, 30 June 1922.

"Chicago's Picture Prosperity." *Variety*, 17 January 1916.

"Chicago's Rialto Faces Changes If Rumors Are True." *Chicago Daily Tribune*, 23 March 1924.

Christiansen, Richard. "Culture, Commerce and Entertainment: Downtown Is Reborn." *Chicago Tribune*, 16 November 1997.

Cinema Treasures. http://cinematreasures.org.

Condit, Carl W. *The Chicago School of Architecture: A History of Commercial and Public Building in the Chicago Area, 1875–1925*. Chicago: University of Chicago Press, 1964.

Crandall, Rick. "Oddities, Rarities and Penny Arcades." www.rickcrandall.net.

"Dime Museums' Glories Dimmed." *Chicago Daily Tribune*, 18 March 1906.

Donaghey, Frederick. "This Thing and That Thing of the Theater." *Chicago Daily Tribune*, 9 May 1926.

Duis, Perry. *Challenging Chicago: Coping with Every Day Life 1837–1920*. Champaign: University of Illinois Press, 1998.

Edwards, Charles. "King Jones Made a Fortune; It Came Nickel by Nickel." *Chicago Daily Tribune*, 11 October 1908.

Ehrenberg, Louis. "Entertaining Chicagoans." In *Encyclopedia of Chicago* (Chicago: Chicago Historical Society, 2004).

Enstad, Robert. "State Street Mall: Amid Chaos, It's on Schedule." *Chicago Tribune*, 10 June 1979.

Estep, George. "Serials Opened a New Chapter in Cinema Adventure." *Chicago Tribune*, 4 May 1986.

"Every Theater in the City Shut by Mayor's Order." *Chicago Daily Tribune*, 3 January 1904.

Eyman, Scott. *The Speed of Sound: Hollywood and the Talkie Revolution, 1926–1930*. New York: Simon & Schuster, 1997.

Fielding, Raymond. *A Technological History of Motion Pictures and Television*. Berkeley: University of California Press, 1967.

Fields, Armond. *Fred Stone*. Jefferson, NC: McFarland, 2002.

"Film Theaters Peril to Public; South State Street Show Houses Lack Adequate Emergency Fire Exits." *Chicago Daily Tribune*, 28 August 1911.

"First Feature Stereo Movie to Open Today." *Chicago Tribune*, 23 January 1953.

"Flats Wrecked; Store Afire." *Chicago Daily Tribune*, 28 April 1909.

Freeburg, Russell. "20th Century's Fortunes Tied to 3-D Movies." *Chicago Tribune*, 3 May 1953.

Gapp, Paul. "Celluloid Cathedrals." *Chicago Tribune*, 9 December, 1984.

_____. "Merchants Optimistic." *Chicago Tribune*, 18 October 1975.

_____. "Now Not Showing." *Chicago Tribune*, 2 July 1989.

Gilbert, Douglas. *American Vaudeville: Its Life and Times*. New York: Dover, 1963.

Goldsborough, Robert. "The Loop (circa 1950): Gawdy, Garish but, Boy, Was It Fun." *Chicago Tribune*, 1 November 1992.

Gomery, Douglas. "Vaudeville." In *Encyclopedia of Chicago* (Chicago: Chicago Historical Society, 2004).

"Good Omen for Show Business: Jones Is Back." *Chicago Daily Tribune*, 23 July 1933.

Gordon, Ruth. "Where Did They All Get Lost?" *Chicago Daily Tribune*, 12 September 1948.

Grinnell, Max. "Going to the Movies." In *Encyclopedia of Chicago* (Chicago: Chicago Historical Society, 2004).

"Hamburger Enterprises Now in New Quarters." *Inter Ocean*, 18 May 1913.

Hammond, Percy. "Edison the Headline in Two Theaters." *Chicago Daily Tribune*, 20 February 1913.

Hatton, Frederic. "A Romance of Chicago Theatricals." *Chicago Daily Tribune*, 30 December 1916.

Hirsley, Michael. "Our Mall 'Totally Ineffective.'" *Chicago Tribune*, 5 October 1980.

History and Architecture of Chicago in Vintage Postcards. www.patsabin.com/illinois/postcardsAZ.htm.

History of film by decade from pre–1920s to present. www.filmsite.org.

"How the Levee Is Encroaching on State Street." *Chicago Daily Tribune*, 2 August 1908.

"Hughes Sells His Holding of RKO Theatres." *Chicago Tribune*, 9 November 1953.

Introduction to the first decade of motion pictures. www.earlycinema.com.

"J. L. & S. Add Two Big Houses to String within Few Days." *Inter Ocean*, 14 December 1913.

Jazz Age: Chicago. http://chicago.urban-history.org.

Jones, Sandra M. "Inside Block 37." *Chicago Tribune*, 15 November 2009.

"Jones, Linick & Schaefer Had a Humble Start." *Inter Ocean*, 14 September 1913.

Kart, Larry. "Old-Time Burlesque Survives and Takes Off with New Zip." *Chicago Tribune*, 3 July 1977.

Knott, Andy. "Past Fade Away under Face Lift." *Chicago Tribune*, 28 October 1979.

"Land Leased for Bigger Morrison." *Chicago Daily Tribune*, 26 May 1911.

"Last Decade of Growth in Chicago in Number of Its Houses." *Chicago Daily Tribune*, 23 November 1910.

Leonard, William. "First Chicago Movie Opened 50 Years Ago." *Chicago Tribune*, 2 October 1955.

_____. "Theater Drought of 1957 City's Longest

of Century." *Chicago Tribune*, 22 September 1957.

Loerzel, Robert. "Reel Chicago." *Chicago Magazine*, May 2007.

Lowe, David Garrard. "Architecture: The First Chicago School." In *Encyclopedia of Chicago* (Chicago: Chicago Historical Society, 2004).

Lukas, Jim. "Mall May Resurrect the Street's Reputation as Entertainment Hub." *Chicago Tribune*, 28 October 1979.

Mabley, Jack. "Memories of State Street." *Chicago Tribune*, 28 October 1979.

"Major Changes in the Works for State Street Mall." *Chicago Tribune*, 16 May 1982.

Manor, Robert. "Vision for the Loop about to Spring forth on Block 37." *Chicago Tribune*, 22 March 2008.

Mather, O. A. "Balaban & Katz Taken Over by Famous Players." *Chicago Daily Tribune*, 7 June 1926.

McIntyre, Robert L. "Behind the Camera — Realism on Film." *Chicago Tribune*, 26 December 1952.

Miller, Ross. "Block 37." In *Encyclopedia of Chicago* (Chicago: Chicago Historical Society, 2004).

Moore, Paul S. *Now Playing: Early Moviegoing and the Regulation of Fun*. Albany: State University of New York Press, 2008.

"Movie Kings Busy in Loop." *Chicago Daily Tribune*, 29 April 1913.

Musser, Charles. *The Emergence of Cinema: The American Screen to 1907*. New York: Scribner, 1990.

"New Chicago." *Chicago Daily Tribune*, 14 April 1872.

"New Morrison Hotel to Cost $2,000,000." *Chicago Daily Tribune*, 10 April 1913.

"Nickel Madness and Bijou Dreams." *Marquee, Journal of the Theatre Historical Society of America* 38, no. 2 (2006).

"The Nickel Theatre Menace." *Chicago Daily Tribune*, 26 December 1908.

"Nickel Theater Pays Well; Small Cost and Big Profit." *Chicago Daily Tribune*, 8 April 1906.

Oleksy, Walter. "What Happens to Chicago's Old Theaters?" *Chicago Tribune*, 5 June 1960.

"On the Rialto in Chicago." *Chicago Daily Tribune*, 13 October 1907.

"Orpheum and Keith-Albee Are Merged." *Chicago Daily Tribune*, 9 December 1927.

Phillips, Michael. "When Chicago Created Hollywood 100 Years Ago." *Chicago Daily Tribune*, 22 July 1907.

Przybylek, Stephanie E. *Breaking the Silence on Film: The History of the Case Research Lab*. Auburn, NY: Cayuga Museum, 1999.

Randall, Frank A., and John D. Randall. *History of the Development of Building Construction in Chicago*. Champaign: University of Illinois Press, 1999.

Ripley, John W. "The Magic Lantern of Bittersweet Tears." *Chicago Tribune*, 29 November 1970.

"RKO Placed in Receivership by Agreement." *Chicago Daily Tribune*, 28 June 1933.

Rosenfeld, Neil. "Art House die — Chicago's Not Even Second Anymore." *Chicago Tribune*, 16 July 1972.

Sawyers, June. "Way We Were." *Chicago Tribune*, 18 June 1989.

"Secret of New Movie System Is Wider Film." *Chicago Tribune*, 15 March 1956.

Shrock, Joel. *The Gilded Age*. Santa Barbara, CA: Greenwood, 2004.

Siry, Joseph M. *The Chicago Auditorium Building: Adler and Sullivan's Architecture and the City*. Chicago: University of Chicago Press, 2004.

Siskel, Gene. "Most of the Kick Comes After the Flick." *Chicago Tribune*, 9 March 1973.

_____. "Movie House Wars: Big 4's Battle to Keep You Coming in High Style." *Chicago Tribune*, 28 October 1984.

_____. "Now Playing: Plitt Theaters." *Chicago Tribune*, 2 June 1974.

_____. "The Public Snuffs out Chain's Chance for a Killing." *Chicago Tribune*, 14 March 1976.

Smith, Sid. "Entertainment Center; How Chicagoans Have Been Amused Since 1847." *Chicago Tribune*, 18 May 1997.

Sorkin, Sidney. "Reel Men: Chicago's Jewish Movie Exhibitors." *Chicago Jewish Historical Society* 25, no. 4 (2001).

South Loop history. www.southloophistory.org.

"State Street Holds Its Charm for Shoppers Thru Constant Change Over the Years." *Chicago Tribune*, 15 July 1956.

"State Street Picture Houses." *Variety*, 19 June 1909.

"State Street to Be Made Canyon of Light." *Chicago Daily Tribune*, 27 August 1925.

Storch, Charles, and Gene Siskel. "Facelift, Expansion for Plitt." *Chicago Daily Tribune*, 28 March 1986.

Teitel, Charles. "Hollywood East — Old Film Row: The Days When the Big Deals Were Cut on South Wabash." *Chicago Tribune*, 16 February 1986.

"Theater 'Trust' Behind Big Deal." *Chicago Daily Tribune*, 4 December 1911.

"Theatres Closed for a Fortnight; Some Houses Must Rebuild." *Chicago Daily Tribune*, 5 January 1904.

"Theatrical Producing Center of the Country." *Chicago Daily Tribune*, 7 February 1909.

Tinee, Mae. "Crowd Sees 'The Robe' Unfurl CinemaScope." *Chicago Tribune*, 24 September 1953.

_____. "New Types of Film Fare." *Chicago Tribune*, 21 March 1954.

Trav S. D. *No Applause, Just Throw Money: The Book That Made Vaudeville Famous*. London: Faber & Faber, 2006.

"Twin Feature Movies Banned in Some Cases." *Chicago Daily Tribune*, 12 November 1947.

"United Artists Theater Goes to Balaban & Katz." *Chicago Daily Tribune*, 2 April 1929.

Vedder, Herbert. "Balaban Made New President of Paramount." *Chicago Daily Tribune*, 3 July 1936.

Wide screen systems, color history, sound development. www.widescreenmuseum.com.

Wiedrich, Bob. "Bringing People Back to the Loop." *Chicago Tribune*, 27 November 1979.

PART II

Abarbanel, Jonathan. "Shubert Goes Back to the Future." *Backstage*, 2 June 2004.

"Adventure at Sea, Scenery Ingredients of Cinemiracle." *Chicago Tribune*, 25 May 1958. (Civic Opera House).

Alcoate, Jack, ed. *Film Daily Yearbooks of Motion Pictures*. New York, 1925–1970.

"The Amazing Return of the Oriental." *Chicago Tribune*, 12 January 1996.

"AMC Closes Acquisition of Loews Cineplex." *USA Today*, 26 January 2006.

"Auditorium Is Bought by College." *Chicago Daily Tribune*, 6 August 1946.

Auditorium Theatre. http://auditoriumtheatre. org.

Bank of America Theatre. www.bankofamerica. theatre.org.

"Bank to Build $3,000,000 Block." *Chicago Daily Tribune*, 28 December 1901. (Haverly's Theatre).

"Bernhardt Honored Here." *Chicago Daily Tribune*, 29 March 1923. (Palace Music Hall).

Bernstein, Arnie. *The Movies Are: Carl Sandburg's Film Reviews and Essays, 1920–1928*. Chicago: Lake Claremont Press, 2000. (Chicago).

"Big RKO Shows Lead Loop." *Chicago Daily Tribune*, 7 June 1930. (Palace).

"Bombs Rock Three Porno Houses; Dynamite Sticks Found in Fourth." *Chicago Tribune*, 15 November 1974.

Brandt, Nat R., Perry Duis, and Cathlyn Schallhorn. *Chicago Death Trap: The Iroquois Theatre Fire of 1903*. Carbondale: Southern Illinois University Press, 2003.

Broadway in Chicago: Chicago's Downtown Theater District. www.BroadwayInChicago.com.

"Building for the Music Folk." *Chicago Daily Tribune*, 2 September 1894. (Steinway Hall).

"Burton Holmes' Third Talk." *Chicago Daily Tribune*, 27 November 1897. (Central Music Hall).

Bushnell, George O. "Chicago's Magnificent Movie Palaces." *Chicago History, Journal of the Chicago Historical Society* 6, no. 2 (1977).

Butler, Sheppard. "Fine Cast in Bold Play at New Adelphi." *Chicago Daily Tribune*, 10 September 1923.

_____. "Loop to Lose Its Oldest Theatres." *Chicago Daily Tribune*, 29 January 1922.

_____. "Theater Notes." *Chicago Daily Tribune*, 18 October 1922.

"Casino Building." *Chicago Daily Tribune*, 23 September 1884. (Brooke's Casino).

Cassidy, Claudia. "Chicago Gets a Theatre for Christmas." *Chicago Tribune*, 3 December 1958.

_____. "On the Aisle," *Chicago Daily Tribune*, 17 October 1945. (Blackstone).

_____. "On the Aisle," *Chicago Tribune*, 22 May 1962. (McVickers).

"Catholic Order Pays $515,000 for Loop Site." *Chicago Daily Tribune*, 12 July 1949. (La Salle).

Caward, Neil G. "The Rise of Jones, Linick & Schaefer." *Motography*, 26 December 1914.

"Central Music Hall Awaits Wreckers." *Chicago Daily Tribune*, 28 April 1901.

Chase, Al. "Apollo Leased for Motion Pictures." *Chicago Daily Tribune*, 28 April 1934.

_____. "Final Curtain Falls for Old Illinois Theater." *Chicago Daily Tribune*, 14 January 1936.

_____. "Lease Majestic Theater to Loop Playhouse Firm." *Chicago Daily Tribune*, 15 March 1934.

_____. "Old Trocadero Theater Sold for $190,000." *Chicago Daily Tribune*, 14 June 1922.

_____. "Oldest Chicago Loop Cinema to Close Doors." *Chicago Daily Tribune*, 13 August 1936.

_____. "Rialto Showhouse to Be Razed." *Chicago Tribune*, 24 November 1953.

_____. "Shuberts Pay Big Premium to Regain Garrick." *Chicago Daily Tribune*, 2 February 1921.

_____. "Shuberts to Lease Pair of New Theaters." *Chicago Daily Tribune*, 26 July 1928.

_____. "Smash Records with Roosevelt Theatre Lease." *Chicago Daily Tribune*, 28 May 1922.

_____. "Warner Bros. Lease Orpheum from J. L. & S." *Chicago Daily Tribune*, 30 June 1925.

Chicago Daily Tribune, 31 August 1879. (Adelphi).

Chicago Daily Tribune, 12 April 1884. (Wood's Museum).

Chicago Daily Tribune, 24 January 1905. (Hyde & Behman's).

Chicago Daily Tribune, 20 January 1909. (American Music Hall).

Chicago Daily Tribune, 8 September 1915. (World).

Chicago Daily Tribune, 14 October 1915. (Bandbox).

Chicago Daily Tribune, 28 September 1919. (Playhouse).

Chicago Daily Tribune, 26 July 1928. (Erlanger).

Chicago Daily Tribune, 12 October 1928. (United Artists).

Chicago Daily Tribune, 6 March 1929. (Rose).

Chicago Daily Tribune, 29 October 1933. (State-Congress).

"Chicago Picture Shows." *Moving Picture World*, 15 July 1911.

"Chicago Theatre." *Theatre Historical Society of America*, annual no. 8, 1981.

Chicago Theatre. www.thechicagotheatre.com.

"Chicago 2003 Conclave Issue, Three Centuries of Theatres." *Marquee, Journal of the Theatre Historical Society of America* 35, no. 1 (2003).

"Chicago's Leading Adult Theatre." *Chicago Tribune*, 4 January 1975. (Cinestage).

"Chief Will Stop Indecent Shows." *Chicago Daily Tribune*, 30 December 1909. (Folly).

Christiansen, Richard. "A Grand Old Movie Palace Finds Itself on Shaky Ground." *Chicago Tribune*, 25 June 1978. (Chicago).

_____. "Celebrating a Great Theater on State Street." *Chicago Tribune*, 21 October 2001.

_____. "Chicago Theatre Books Comeback." *Chicago Tribune*, 8 April 1986.

_____. "Chicago Theatre Faces a Tough Comeback Fight." *Chicago Tribune*, 11 September 1988.

_____. "Stage Set for Glittering Comeback by Oriental." *Chicago Tribune*, 11 January 1996.

_____. "World Playhouse Ready to Return to Arts Action." *Chicago Tribune*, 18 September 1980.

"Cinemiracle — It's Done with Mirrors." *Chicago Tribune*, 8 June 1958. (Civic Opera House).

Civic Opera House. www.civicoperahouse.com.

"Civic Theater Will Become Video Studio." *Chicago Daily Tribune*, 29 August 1948.

"Cohan's Grand Opera House to Be Wrecked; Plan New One." *Chicago Daily Tribune*, 20 June 1925.

Collins, Charles. "Chicago Gets Play of Home Grown Variety." *Chicago Daily Tribune*, 19 September 1932.

_____. "Cort Theatre Surrenders to Drama Famine." *Chicago Daily Tribune*, 7 October 1934.

_____. "Movie Theater Will Offer Old Globe Players." *Chicago Daily Tribune*, 9 November 1934. (McVickers).

_____. "Play Supply Greater Than Rialto Space." *Chicago Daily Tribune*, 19 September 1937. (Erlanger).

_____. "Stage Landmark Becomes Park Place." *Chicago Daily Tribune*, 9 June 1935. (State-Congress).

"Col. John Hopkins Showman Is Dead." *Chicago Daily Tribune*, 25 October 1909. (Hopkins).

"Columbia and Star & Garter Are Attacked." *Chicago Daily Tribune*, 28 August 1921.

"Dangerous Crowding of Theatres." *Chicago Daily Tribune*, 25 January 1879. (Haverly's).

"Discover Long Hidden Art in Garrick Relics." *Chicago Tribune*, 26 July 1961.

Duis, Perry R. "Where Is Athens Now? The Fine Arts Building 1898 to 1918." *Chicago History, Journal of the Chicago Historical Society of America* 6, no. 2 (1977).

"The East Side of State Street." *Chicago Daily Tribune*, 30 March 1883. (Park Theatre).

"Eight Years of Popularity for Student Prince." *Chicago Daily Tribune*, 12 February 1933. (Great Northern).

"End of an Era." *Chicago Tribune*, 15 June 1970.

"The End of Central Music Hall." *Chicago Daily Tribune*, 28 April 1901.

"The End of the Rialto Burlesque." *Life Magazine*, 18 September 1944.

"Enter — New McVicker's." *Chicago Daily Tribune*, 22 March 1891.

"Events of a City Day." *Chicago Daily Tribune*, 25 March 1896. (Park Theatre).

Famed Old Orpheum Theater Will Give Way to Shoe Store." *Chicago Daily News*, 8 March 1937.

"Famed Old Princess Theater Yields to the Ax of Wreckers." *Chicago Daily Tribune*, 12 July 1941.

"Farrar's Carmen Opens New Strand." *Chicago Daily Tribune*, 16 October 1915.

"Film Coup Ends Famous Player Theater Rumor." *Chicago Daily Tribune*, 9 July 1922. (McVickers).

Fine Arts Theatres. www.fineartsbuilding.tv.

"French Film to Open New Capri Theater Friday." *Chicago Tribune*, 29 June 1958.

"Gem Theater Girl Dancer Answers Woman Accuser." *Chicago Daily Tribune*, 2 February 1916.

Gene Siskel Film Center. www.siskelfilmcenter. org.

The Gettysburg Cyclorama. www.gettysburg.edu /special_collections/contact.dot; www.nps.gov/ gett/historyculture/gettysburg-cyclorama.htm.

"Girls Take-Em Off For Last Time at Rialto." *Chicago Tribune*, 1 January 1954.

"Give City Theater Palace." *Chicago Daily Tribune*, 14 July 1909.

"Good Omens in New Career of Old Auditorium." *Chicago Daily Tribune*, 2 April 1933.

"The Goodman Picks a Perfect Spot." *Chicago Tribune*, 8 January 1992.

Goodman Theatre. www.goodmantheatre.org.

"Hails New Oriental as Wonder Theater." *Chicago Daily News*, 8 May 1926.

"Hamlin's New Theatre." *Chicago Daily Tribune*, 9 May 1880.

Hammond, Percy. "Blackstone Opens, Beauty Praised." *Chicago Daily Tribune*, 1 January 1911.

_____. "Concerning the New Columbia." *Chicago Daily Tribune*, 27 February 1911.

Heiser, John. "The Gettysburg Cyclorama." In *Gettysburg National Military Park* (National Park Service, December 2005).

Henning, Joel. "Form Follows Function, Elegantly." *Wall Street Journal*, 6 September 2008. (Auditorium).

"History of the Famous Theater." *Chicago Daily Tribune*, 27 August 1890. (McVicker's).

Hubbard, W.L. "News of the Theaters." *Chicago Daily Tribune*, 23 November 1908. (Garden Theatre).

_____. "News of the Theaters." *Chicago Daily Tribune*, 10 June 1945. (Majestic).

"Huge Building May Supplant Strand Theater." *Chicago Daily Tribune*, 26 June 1921.

Hutchinson, Louise. "Finale Stirs Fond Memories of Old Grand." *Chicago Tribune*, 1 April 1958.

"Illinois Theater to Be Ready tor Opening on Oct. 1." *Chicago Daily Tribune*, 16 January 1900.

Indreika, Jim G. "The History of the Schiller (Garrick) Theatre." *Marquee, The Journal of the Theatre Historical Society of America* 30, no. 3 (1998).

"Inter Ocean Building Will Be Movie House." *Chicago Daily Tribune*, 8 January 1919. (Monroe).

Inter Ocean Morning News, 2 March 1913. (Orpheum).

"Iroquois Feels Memory of Fire." *Chicago Daily Tribune*, 29 December 1904.

"Iroquois Is Open." *Chicago Daily Tribune*, 2 September 1904.

"It Is Completely Fireproof." *Chicago Daily Tribune*, 30 September 1892. (Schiller).

Jones, Chris. "Chicago Theatre to Be Sold to Major New York Producer." *Chicago Tribune*, 9 October 2007.

_____. "Chicago's Fine Arts Building: New Life For the Studebaker and the Playhouse." *Chicago Tribune*, 15 January 2008.

_____. "Historic Studebaker Gets Another Moment in the Spotlight." *Chicago Tribune*, 11 August 2008.

"Joys of Amateur Night at the Folly Theater." *Chicago Daily Tribune*, 17 February 1907.

Kamin, Blair. "They Don't Build 'Em Like This Any More." *Chicago Tribune*, 11 February 1996.

Kelly, Kitty. "Chicagoans See Novel Film Show." *Chicago Daily Tribune*, 1 May 1915. (Orchestra Hall).

_____. "Flickerings From Filmland." *Chicago Daily Tribune*, 18 October 1915. (Olympic Theatre).

_____. "Flickerings from Filmland." *Chicago Daily Tribune*, 2 May 1916. (Castle).

Kogan, Rick. "Revisiting Chicago's Rialto." *Chicago Tribune*, 5 October 1986.

Leonard, William. "Wreckers Uncover Theater Nostalgia." *Chicago Tribune*, 5 April 1970. (Central).

Levin, Meyer. *The Old Bunch*. n.p.: Greenwood, 1937. (Chicago).

"Loop Theater Released from Two Feature Curb." *Chicago Daily Tribune*, 21 November 1947. (McVickers).

"Mayor Harrison Visits Levee District and Closes Variety Shows." *New York Times*, 30 September 1911.

McQuade, James S. "Picture Row." *Film Index*, 20 August 1910.

"McVickers Will Show Oklahoma Film on December 26." *Chicago Tribune*, 6 November 1955.

"Minsky Takes Over Rialto Theater Friday." *Chicago Tribune*, 23 April 1950.

"Miss Ethel Barrymore to Be at Palace." *Chicago Daily Tribune*, 4 August 1933.

Moore, Edward. "Romeo and Juliet to Close Opera in Auditorium." *Chicago Daily Tribune*, 8 January 1929.

_____. "Totally Deaf Can Hear at This Theater." *Chicago Daily Tribune*, 29 March 1935. (Sonotone).

Morris, Charles F. "Example of Modern Theater Construction." *The Nickelodeon*, 1 January 1910.

Naylor, David, and Joan Dillon. *American Theaters: Performance Halls of the Nineteenth Century*. New York: Wiley, 1997.

"New Chicago Film Palace Opening Draws Great Throngs." *Billboard*, 5 November 1921.

"New Chicago: Notes of Progress: Condition of Affairs in the Three Divisions." *Chicago Daily Tribune*, 14 April 1872. (McVicker's and Aiken's theatres).

"New German War Films Tomorrow." *Chicago Daily Tribune*, 21 July 1916.

"New Music Hall." *Chicago Daily Tribune*, 10 August 1879.

"New Playhouse for Clark Street." *Chicago Daily Tribune*, 9 November 1907. (Princess).

Newman, M. W. "A Former Flapper Roars to Life, The Oriental Returns to Its 1920s Glory." *Chicago Tribune*, 15 October 1998.

"News of the Theaters." *Chicago Daily Tribune*, 2 September 1899.

"News of the Theaters." *Chicago Daily Tribune*, 4 October 1913. (Comedy).

"Old Inter-Ocean Building to Be Made Theatre." *Chicago Daily Tribune*, 20 May 1918.

"The Only Cinerama Theatre within 300 Miles." *Chicago Tribune*, 16 July 1955.

"Opening of Big Loop House Only Week Away." *Chicago Evening American*, 1 May 1926. (Oriental).

Orchestra Hall. www.cso.org.

"The Oriental Theatre, Chicago." *Theatre Historical Society of America*, annual no. 24, 1997.

"Oriental Theater Is sold." *Chicago Tribune*, 18 November 1978.

Patner, Andrew. "Restoration Drama: Theatre-Dreams Determined to Revive Chicago Stage." *Chicago Sun-Times*, 28 March 2004.

"Play and Playhouse Scored Successes." *Chicago Daily Tribune*, 26 October 1909. (Cort).

"Playbills." *Chicago Daily Tribune*, 16 June 1905. (Hyde & Behman's).

Pratt, Steven. "McVickers Theater to Close Tomorrow." *Chicago Tribune*, 17 May 1971.

"Pride Is Held Last Hope of the Garrick." *Chicago Tribune*, 7 July 1960.

"Quacks Driven Out of Chicago." *Chicago Daily Tribune*, 24 April 1915. (Folly).

Remisoff, Nicolas. "The Punch and Judy Theatre." *Western Architect*, November 1930.

"Reopening of the People's Theatre." *Chicago Daily Tribune*, 11 February 1894.

"Rialto Loses a Landmark." *Chicago Daily Tribune*, 18 May 1924. (Colonial).

"Rialto Theater Brings Shows from New York." *Chicago Daily Tribune*, 30 August 1936.

"Roosevelt Theater to Be Opened Today." *Chicago Daily Tribune*, 23 April 1921.

"A Rose Pink Music Hall." *Chicago Daily Tribune*, 11 November 1908. (Olympic Theatre).

Roth, Leland M. *A Concise History of American Architecture*. New York: Harper & Row, 1980.

"Show Managers Now Face Arrest." *Chicago Daily Tribune*, 2 July 1908.

Siskel, Gene. "Chicago Theater to Close September 19 for Renovation." *Chicago Tribune*, 8 September 1985.

_____. "Famed Oriental Theater Will Close as Film House." *Chicago Tribune*, 9 December 1980.

_____. "The Little Giant of the Loop." *Chicago Tribune*, 21 May 1972. (Loop).

_____. "M&R Will Add 3rd Screen to Fine Arts." *Chicago Tribune*, 24 November 1983.

_____. "Rating the New Multiplexes." *Chicago Tribune*, 14 September 1984. (Fine Arts Theatres).

_____. "Roosevelt Theater Will Close Sept. 1." *Chicago Tribune*, 31 July 1979.

_____. "Show's Over for Todd Theatre." *Chicago Tribune*, 14 April 1977.

_____. "State-Lake Curtain Falls on June 28." *Chicago Tribune*, 19 June 1984.

_____. "Todd, Cinestage Theaters Getting New Lease on Life." *Chicago Tribune*, 3 November 1985.

"Six Loop Theatres Shut." *Chicago Tribune*, 23 January 1975.

Sjostrom, Joseph. "Follies, a Shady Lady of Theater, Dies in Fire." *Chicago Tribune*, 5 January 1978.

Smith, Cecil. "Play First of Popular Priced Attractions Planned for City." *Chicago Daily Tribune*, 4 April 1943. (Studebaker).

"Starts a Riot at the Savoy." *Chicago Daily Tribune*, 25 November 1898.

"State Street Theaters Get Consent of Women Who Closed Them Up." *Chicago Daily Tribune*, 24 February 1916.

"State Street Theatres." *Variety*, 19 June 1909.

"Theater Burns; Crowd Is Calm." *Chicago Daily Tribune*, 29 December 1901. (Park).

"Theater Notes." *Chicago Daily Tribune*, 14 December 1922. (Aryan Grotto).

"Theaters to Make Changes to Comply with City Laws." *Chicago Daily Tribune*, 25 June 1908.

Tinee, Mae. "Another Star Portrayal Given by Rin-Tin-Tin." *Chicago Daily Tribune*, 26 September 1927. (Majestic).

_____. "Castle Theater Goes Back to Feature Films." *Chicago Daily Tribune*, 25 May 1932.

_____. "Crowds Stand in Line to Hear First Talkie." *Chicago Daily Tribune*, 4 August 1928. (McVickers).

_____. "Jane Eyre Film to Open Regime at McVickers." *Chicago Daily Tribune*, 3 December 1934.

_____. "Jolson Magic Is Magic Still, Even in Movie." *Chicago Daily Tribune*, 1 December 1927. (Garrick).

_____. "Movies." *Chicago Tribune*, 29 March 1953. (World Playhouse).

_____. "Refurbishing of 'Flagship' Is Completed." *Chicago Tribune*, 1 November 1953. (Chicago).

_____. "Right Off the Reel." *Chicago Daily Tribune*, 22 December 1918. (Randolph).

_____. "Theater Man Reports on the New 3-D Films." *Chicago Tribune*, 12 April 1953. (Chicago).

_____. "This Is Cinerama Returns." *Chicago Tribune*, 18 June 1961. (Palace).

_____. "'Wings' Is Brilliant, Poignant, and in Spots 'Most Too Real." *Chicago Daily Tribune*, 1 November 1927. (Erlanger).

"Tivoli and Chicago Theatres Eightieth Anniversary Tribute." *Marquee, The Journal of the Theatre Historical Society of America* 33, no. 3 (2001).

"Tower Ticker." *Chicago Daily Tribune*, 18 October 1949. (Telenews).

"Twenty Years Ago on State Street Rialto." *Chicago Daily Tribune*, 10 September 1933. (State-Lake).

"Vandals Invade Theater; Ruin 'Improper' Film." *Chicago Daily Tribune*, 7 September 1949.

"Vaudeville at Palace, Chicago, and State-Lake." *Chicago Daily Tribune*, 10 September 1933.

"Vaudeville Takes Colonial; to Open at 10, 15, 25 Cents." *Chicago Daily Tribune*, 10 May 1913.

Wagenknecht, Edward. "When Movies Cost Five Cents, Lasted 30 Minutes." *Chicago Tribune*, 9 December 1962. (Hale's Tours).

Wiedrich, Robert. "Enchantment of Wood's Museum Recalled." *Chicago Tribune*, 8 July 1951.

"Wilson Boosts Play That Will Open Theater." *Chicago Daily Tribune*, 6 March 1918. (Woods).

"Wrecking Crews Dropped the Final Curtain." *Chicago Tribune*, 8 April 1958. (RKO Grand Theatre).

Ziemba, Stanley. "Two Theaters Regain 'Must-Save' Status." *Chicago Tribune*, 15 October 1982.

Index

Numbers in **_bold italics_** indicate pages with photographs.